Apples,
Bean Dip,
and
Carrot Cake

Kids! Teach Yourself to Cook

Anne and Freya Dinshah

Parents approved their children's participation, with use of photographs and names, in this project.

The information contained herein is for educational purposes. Children must consult responsible adults prior to performing the tasks described. The authors and publisher disclaim all liability in connection with use of this book. Parents and other supervising adults are responsible for watching children work safely. A ratio of one adult to one child is recommended.

First edition: November 2012
ISBN: 978-0-942401-22-6

Published by:
American Vegan Society
56 Dinshah Lane, PO Box 369
Malaga NJ 08328 U.S.A.

Printed in the United States of America

Cover and book design by Anne Dinshah and Carol Githens. All food and children's photos by Anne Dinshah. Authors' photo by Jayteck Professional Services.

Thank you to all who read the manuscript and offered comments, corrections, and encouragement, especially Janelle Davidson, Wenona Dege, Jal J. Dinshah, Lois Dinshah, Carol Githens, Emily Mingin, Rosemary O'Brien, Stephanie Salazar, and Marietta Webster.

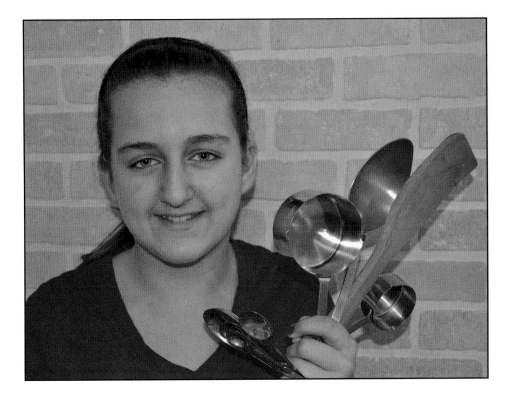

Dedicated to Emily Mingin

who tested and edited every recipe at age 10

Acknowledgments

Many thanks to everyone who invented, tested, and tasted recipes, especially:

Kiara Bowen

Jeremy and Matthew Dege

Clint Dinshah

Kyle and Ashley Dinshah

Zachary and Joshua Dinshah

Amanda and Carli Hullihen

AnaMichele Morejon

Monica and Michael Parson

Emily and Charles Roth

Cheyenne Sadowski

Eric and Benjamin Schmalzried

Ruthanne and Matthew Swartz

Ava West

and many anonymous little helpers

Amanda, 10   Ashley, 5

Ava, 3

Ben, 7

The chefs pictured will help you learn throughout the book.

Carli, 6

Charlie, 7

Cheyenne, 11

Clint, 1

Emily R, 9

Eric, 9

Jeremy, 11

Josh, 6

Kiara, 11

Kyle, 11

Matthew S, 3

Michael, 8

Monica, 12

Ruthie, 5

Zach, 10

Contents

Recipes listed in regular print and *How-to pages in italics*

Contents

Contents

Contents

Introduction

Apples, Bean Dip, and Carrot Cake is designed for children ages four through twelve to make simple, healthful recipes — even when a child is the only person in the home fond of kitchen tasks. No experience is necessary. This book will also appeal to some adults.

Kids should ask adults to watch them work safely as each new skill is learned. Ability develops quickly and the results are delicious. When they have completed this book, kids will be able to tackle recipes in basic adult cookbooks.

Although an occasional demonstration may be helpful, adults should resist the urge to jump in and do the recipe. Allow kids ample time to learn from the hands-on experience.

How to Use This Book

Always work safely and focus on each task. **Follow the steps in order.** Those with more experience may skip recipes but should read through them to be familiar with all the processes; especially note directions in a blue box.

Recipes list all the required equipment and ingredients. The number on each photo matches the number of a direction in the recipe. A letter "I" indicates a photo showing ingredients. An "S" is a serving suggestion. Sometimes a "How to" section details a specific step.

This book will stay open while you work because it is made with a lay-flat binding. Gently press the spine open. To easily read the book and keep it clean, place the book close to where you will be working but not on your work surface.

There are four levels. When you have successfully completed each level, go to pages 157 or 159 at the end of the book for your certificate of accomplishment!

Working in the Kitchen: Setup and Cleanup

Plan Ahead

Ask an adult for permission to use the kitchen, and show the adult the recipe you plan to use. Read the whole recipe. Skills build on each other; if you don't remember how to do something, refer to previous pages, or ask for help. Make sure all ingredients are on hand or write a shopping list. Check that you have all the equipment needed too.

Since you have approved kitchen time, there should not be any people disrupting your work. If you are good at cooperative cooking, confirm with the adult that your assistant is also approved for the kitchen. There is never arguing or horseplay allowed in the kitchen. Everyone needs room to work.

Get Ready

Tie up long hair or put it under a hat. Keep pets out of the kitchen. Wear clean play clothes or an apron. Short sleeves are good because they stay out of the way of your work.

If you are not tall enough to reach the sink or counter comfortably, use a **stepstool** with all feet of the stool firmly planted on the floor.

Make sure **work spaces are clean and tidy** before starting the recipe.

Always **wash your hands** with soap and warm water before working with food. Get your hands wet; put a drop of soap on them. Rub hands together while singing the Happy Birthday song (about 10 seconds). Then rinse them under running water while singing the song again.

Sometimes **rinsing hands** is in the directions. Rinsing is just running water over your hands to remove food from them before returning to your work.

Follow the Recipe step by step in order. Read whole recipe first. Reread one numbered step. Then read and do one sentence at a time.

Serve fabulous creations with pride! Serving suggestions often appear at the end of recipes.

Cleanup: If you spill, then wipe it up immediately. Clean up completely when you are finished. This includes washing all equipment and dishes. Clean work surfaces. Put away unused ingredients. Each section teaches new cleanup skills.

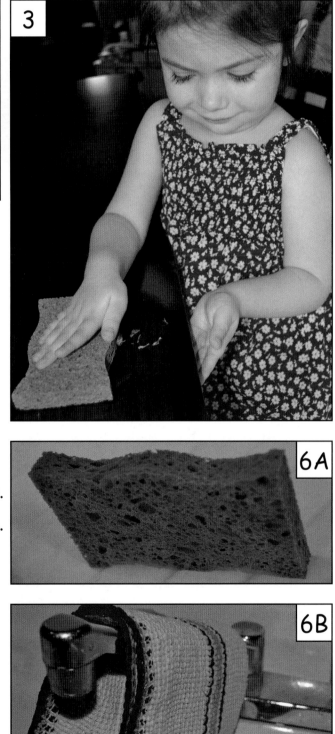

How to Clean Up a Work Surface (Table or Counter)

1. Wet a clean sponge or dishcloth.
2. Wring it out with a twist.
3. Wipe the table, carefully pulling any bits into a pile. Then hold your hand or a bowl under the tabletop edge and wipe bits into it.
4. Shake bits into compost or garbage.
5. Rinse and wring sponge or dishcloth.
6. Set sponge on edge so it will dry (A), or hang up the dishcloth (B).

Compost is food scraps such as parts of fruits and vegetables that you don't eat, but will decompose and fertilize a garden.

Washing Dishes

One or two dishes:

1. If there are any large pieces of food left on the dish, use a utensil to scrape the food into the compost container.

2. At the sink, wet a sponge or dishcloth and put a drop of dish soap on it.

3. Wipe sponge all over the dish, holding it carefully because it will be slippery. When finished, rinse clean and wring out the sponge.

4. Rinse dish under hot water. Do not burn yourself; very warm is okay.

5. Put dish in a dish rack to dry.

Large pile of dirty dishes:

Ask if you can use the dishwasher OR wash dishes by hand: Fill a sink with soapy water for washing, then rinse. You can ask someone to share the fun (wash or rinse) on this big job.

Can you find this equipment in your kitchen?

Items will be used later in this book.

blender

can opener

cookie cutters

baking sheet

colander

baking pan

frying pan

cooling rack

citrus juicers

grater

whisk

chef's knife

serrated knife

ice cream scoops

paring knife

fork   spoon

mashers

table knife

ladle

dry measuring cups set

measuring spoons set

liquid measuring cup

mixing bowl

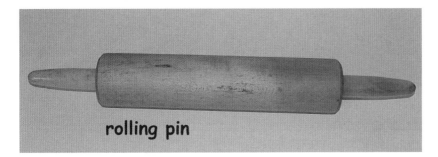
rolling pin

pot holders

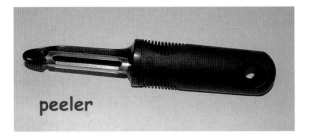
peeler

large pot

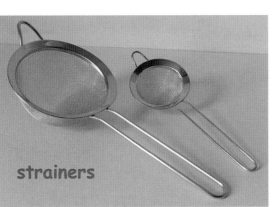
oven mitts

small pot

strainers

serving spoons

wooden spoons

stove

oven

steamer basket

lifting spatulas

scraping spatulas

sushi mat

timer

vegetable scrub brush

tongs

towels

Level One: Let's Begin

APPLE

Yield: 1 serving

Skill learned: washing

Equipment: 1 paper towel

Ingredient: 1 apple

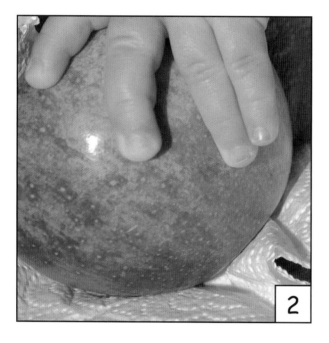

Directions:

1. Turn on water at sink. Rub apple in water with your hands while counting to ten. Turn off water.

2. Rub apple with paper towel to make it clean, dry, and shiny.

3. Bite the apple. Chew.

4. Discard the core and seeds, preferably in the compost.

GRAPES

Yield: 2 servings   **Equipment:** large bowl, colander

Skill learned: washing   **Ingredient:** 1 bunch grapes

Directions:

1. Place grapes in the bowl. Put bowl in the sink.
2. Fill bowl with cool water. Gently swish grapes in the water.
3. Place colander in the sink. Move grapes to colander. Empty water from the bowl into the sink.
4. Pluck individual grapes and eat.

TRAIL MIX

Yield: 2 servings

Skills learned: elementary measuring, sharing, closing resealable bag

Equipment: 1 resealable plastic bag

Ingredients:

1 handful cashew nuts

2 handfuls raisins

3 handfuls toasted whole grain oat cereal

Directions:

1. Open plastic bag. Place bag on table or counter.
2. Put 1 handful of cashews in the bag.
3. Add 2 handfuls of raisins.
4. Add 3 handfuls of cereal.
5. Close the bag by pinching the sealing strips together and rubbing fingers along to feel it seal. Strips may be pressed against the table with fingers to help it close. Carefully turn bag upside down to make sure it is closed.
6. Hold one corner of the bag. Shake the bag. Hold opposite corner. Shake.
7. Open the bag. Share with a friend.

Variety Trail Mix

Ingredients may be added or substituted. In place of raisins, try chopped dried pineapple, dried mango pieces, or sliced dried bananas. In place of cashews try almonds, hazelnuts (filberts), walnuts, peanuts, shelled sunflower seeds, or pumpkin seeds.

RIPPED SALAD

Yield: 1 serving

Skills learned: washing leaves, ripping

Equipment: large bowl, small bowl

Ingredients:

2 lettuce leaves, any leafy variety

3 spinach leaves

4 grape tomatoes or cherry tomatoes

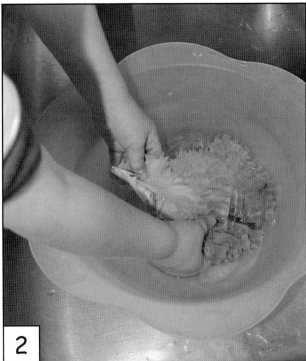

Directions:

1. Put large bowl in sink. Fill with cool water.

2. Use your hands to swish one leaf in the water. Rub your fingers along leaf under water to unfold crinkles and loosen dirt. Shake water off leaf.

3. Pinch leaf with both hands and rip apart (or let a friend help rip) until you have bite-sized pieces. Place pieces in small bowl.

4. Repeat steps 2 and 3 with remaining leaves.

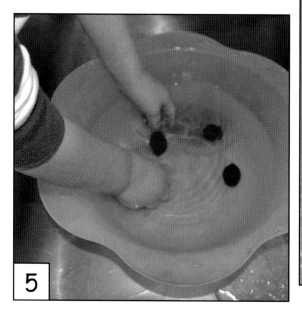

5. Put tomatoes in bowl of water and swish. Place tomatoes in small bowl.

6. Empty the water from the large bowl into the sink.

Serving: with *Shake-It Dressing* (p. 38).

Q: What would happen if you wash lettuce in hot water?

Q: Can you name some leafy varieties of lettuce?

A: It would wilt.

A: Romaine, red leaf, green leaf, Boston, bibb, buttercrunch.

COOL BLUE TREAT

Yield: 1 serving

Skills learned: counting, layering

Equipment: small glass, spoon

Ingredients:

40 frozen blueberries

1 small container vanilla soy yogurt (6 ounces)

    or take 3/4 cup from larger container

Directions:

1. Count 12 blueberries into a glass.

2. Spoon soy yogurt to just cover berries in the glass.

3. Place another 20 berries on the yogurt in the glass.

4. Add soy yogurt to cover berries again.

5. Top with 8 berries in any pattern you choose. Eat before the berries thaw.

How to Freeze Blueberries

Equipment: big bowl, colander, resealable plastic bag

Ingredient: Blueberries

1. Put the big bowl in the sink. Fill it half way with water.
2. Put blueberries into bowl. Swish berries with your hands.
3. Put colander in sink.

   Take one handful of blueberries. As you put them in the colander, remove any rotten (squishy) berries, unripe berries, or stems. Repeat with remaining berries.
4. Shake colander over the sink to remove water from berries. Let them dry at least 5 minutes.

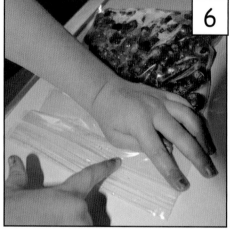

5. Place bag on counter. Hold the bag open with one hand. Use other hand to put berries in bag.
6. Gently remove air from the bag by pressing the empty part against the counter. Press sealing strips together to close. Place bag in freezer.

Notes: If the bag is not self-sealing, twist the top end of the bag to close. Wrap a twist tie around the closure and twist the tie until it holds. Alternatively, a clothespin can be opened and pinched onto the closure. Berries should be used within a year of when they are frozen.

SOAKED APRICOTS

Yield: 2 servings

Skill learned: soaking

Equipment: small container with lid

Ingredients:

6 dried apricots

water

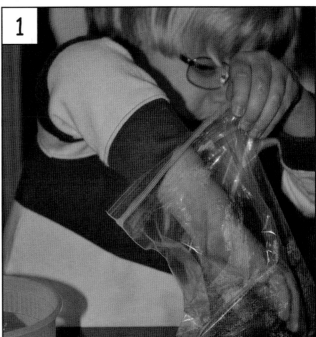

Directions:

1. Take apricots from storage bag and place in container.
2. Put water in container. There should be half an inch (1/2") of water above the apricots.
3. Cover container with lid. Leave overnight on counter.

Serving: In the morning, spoon half of the apricots and juice into another cup. Eat apricots with a spoon in the company of a friend.

Mini math: When you divide 6 apricots between 2 cups, how many apricots are in each? If you divide 6 apricots among 3 cups, how many are in each?

A: 3, 2

COLD HERB TEA

Yield: 2 1/2 cups

Skills learned: steeping (soaking an object in liquid), opening and closing jar, telling time

Equipment: one 2 1/2-cup-sized jar with lid (clean recycled)

Ingredients:

cold water

1 herb tea bag, such as a flavor containing rose hips and hibiscus

Directions:

1. Place jar on table. Hold jar with one hand. Use other hand to remove lid with a left twist (counterclockwise).

2. Fill jar almost to the top with cold water.

3. Do NOT open tea bag. Place tea bag in jar.

4. Secure lid with a right twist (clockwise).

5. Watch tea begin to steep. Then set in refrigerator for 4 hours.

6. Take jar out of refrigerator and place on table. Open jar. Remove tea bag and hold just above jar. Squeeze tea out of bag.

Serving: Pour into glasses and serve. It should be refreshing and a bit tart.

Practice Measuring

Practice pouring and measuring liquids

Pouring and measuring liquids should be done outdoors or on a tray.

Lightweight plastic wet measuring cups are safer for kids than glass.

Equipment: 2 liquid measuring cups, measuring spoons set, tray (if indoors)

Ingredient: water

Directions:

Pouring

1. Set tray on counter (indoors) or find a level area to work outdoors.

2. Fill one liquid measuring cup with water to the top measuring line,

below the top edge. Place second liquid measuring cup on tray.

3. Slowly pour water from first measuring cup into the second and back again.

Q: Why are there different measuring cups for liquid and dry ingredients?

A: When you are carrying liquid, a dry measuring cup filled to the top with liquid would spill.
For dry ingredients it is easier to measure accurately by sweeping across the top with a knife to level it.

Measuring liquids

Practice stopping water at each line of the measuring cup such as 1/4, 1/3, 1/2, 2/3, 3/4, 1 cup: Have your eyes at the level of a line and look across while pouring. If you need more, continue pouring. If you have too much, pour some back into the original cup.

Practice measuring small amounts of liquid

1. Dip a measuring spoon into a measuring cup full of water, keeping the spoon level. The spoon should be full. Pour water from the spoon into the other cup. Repeat process with different size spoons.

2. When the water in the cup becomes too low to fill a spoon, gently tilt the cup.

3. When the water is too low to fill a spoon by tilting, hold spoon over the tray and pour water from the cup into the spoon.

Practice measuring dry ingredients

Equipment: dry measuring cup set, measuring spoons set, table knife, tray or plate, spoon

Ingredients: any dry food in small pieces such as salt, rice, flour, or sugar
For outdoor play at the beach, practice with sand. (Do not eat.)

1. Practice filling dry measuring cups: Place one dry measuring cup on the tray. Scoop salt (or other ingredient) with spoon into measuring cup or pour it in. Do not scoop directly with the measuring cup because it will pack and not be accurate. Allow salt to heap slightly on top.

2. Place back (straight) edge of knife across top of the dry measuring cup. Move knife across the cup to level the salt. High spots move to fill low spots. Excess falls on the tray. Add more salt if needed. Do not bang cup on table to level top because that can pack it and not be accurate.

3. Repeat with different size measuring cups. Practice pouring contents of smaller cups into larger ones and add amounts such as 1/4 + 1/4 = 1/2 cup OR 1/4 +1/4 + 1/2 = 1 cup OR 1/3 + 1/3 + 1/3 = 1 cup.

Practice measuring small amounts of dry ingredients

1. Dip a measuring spoon into salt. Hold measuring spoon over tray.

2. Level the top with the back of the table knife. Some containers have a top piece that can level the spoon as you pull it out of the container.

3. Add amounts such as 3 teaspoons equal 1 tablespoon.

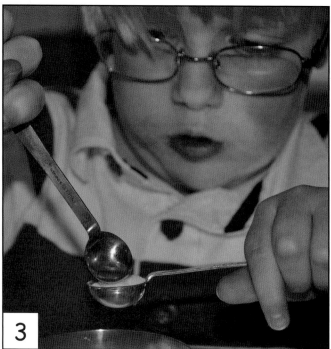

PUNCH

Yield: 2 cups

Skills learned: opening and closing bottle, pouring, wet measuring

Equipment: tray or towel, liquid measuring cup (2-cup size)

Ingredients:

1 cup fruit juice

1 cup seltzer water

Directions:

1. Place tray on work surface (table or counter). Place measuring cup on tray. Put juice and seltzer bottles on the work surface.

2. Grasp juice bottle with one hand. With your other hand, open bottle by turning the lid counterclockwise.

3. Slowly pour juice into measuring cup to the 1-cup line. Close juice bottle by twisting the lid on clockwise.

4. Open seltzer bottle. Slowly add seltzer water to juice in measuring cup to the two-cup line. Close seltzer bottle.

Serving: Put glasses on tray. Pour punch into glasses.

Notes: The tray catches spills or towel soaks up spills. When confident at pouring, they become unnecessary. Tray is preferred because the spill can be drunk with a straw and the tray can easily be washed. In doing this recipe for the first time, it is easier to work from small or half-full bottles.

FRUIT JUICE POPSICLES

Yield: 3 servings

Skill learned: freezing

Equipment: aluminum foil, ruler, scissors, 3 small paper cups, tray, 3 food-grade craft sticks, plastic plate

Ingredient: fruit juice

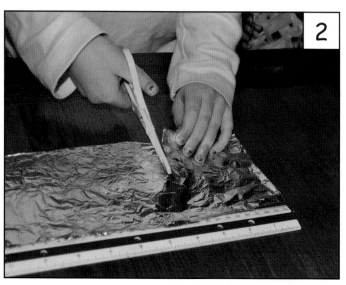

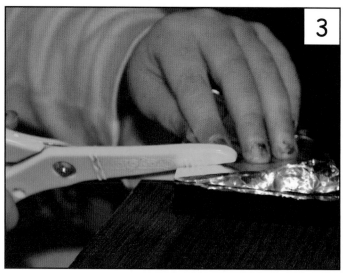

Directions:

1. Unroll enough aluminum foil to be able to cut one strip 4 inches wide. Use scissors and ruler to measure and cut the strip of aluminum foil.

2. Cut strip into three 4-inch squares.

3. Fold each square in half and cut a tiny slit in the middle of the fold.

4. Place cups on tray. Pour juice into each cup until 3/4-full.

5. Cover each cup with a square of aluminum foil.

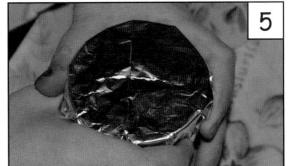

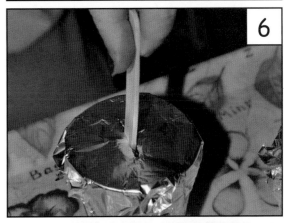

6. Place a craft stick through slit into each cup.

7. Put plastic plate in freezer, level on a shelf where it will not be disturbed. Carefully set each cup on the plate. Be sure to close freezer door. Freeze overnight or at least 4 hours.

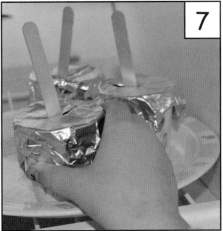

Serving: Check that popsicle is frozen solid. Take popsicle from freezer and set on counter until popsicle edge thaws enough for popsicle to come out of cup (about 5 minutes, depending on weather) OR you may hold the popsicle upside down under hot running water to loosen. Pull popsicle from cup and lick. Eat outdoors or use a large napkin to catch drips.

SHAKE-IT DRESSING

Yield: 1/2 cup

Skills learned: precise liquid measuring, precise dry measuring, shaking

Equipment: jar with well-fitting lid — at least 1-cup size, liquid measuring cup, tray, small bowl, measuring spoons set

Ingredients:

1/4 cup olive oil

2 Tablespoons apple juice

1 Tablespoon lemon juice or vinegar

1/2 teaspoon mixed dried herbs

1/8 teaspoon salt

Directions:

1. Unscrew the lid from the jar.

2. Place tray on a level surface such as the counter. Place liquid measuring cup on the tray. Have your eyes even with the measuring mark you are using. Pour oil into liquid measuring cup very slowly until it reaches the 1/4-cup line. Pour the 1/4 cup oil into the jar.

3. Pour some apple juice into the small bowl. Dip the tablespoon into the apple juice to fill the tablespoon. Pour tablespoon of apple juice into jar. Refill tablespoon and pour into jar. You may drink apple juice that remains in the bowl.

4. Place tablespoon on the tray. You may need to support the handle on the edge of the tray to keep it level. Pour lemon juice from container into tablespoon. Put lemon juice into jar.

5. Fill 1/2 teaspoon measure with dried herbs until the top is level. Add to jar.

6. Put salt in the 1/8 teaspoon measure (or half-fill a 1/4 teaspoon). Add to jar.

7. Replace lid on jar. Make sure it is tightly sealed. Turn upside down slowly to be sure it does not leak.

8. Hold jar firmly in both hands. Shake well until dressing looks evenly mixed.

Serving: Open jar. Use teaspoon to put small amount of dressing onto a salad such as *Ripped Salad*.

Level Two:
Using Knives
and
Other Tools

knives, can opener, masher, citrus juicer,
salad spinner, peeler, and grater

Safe Cleanup and Table Setting

How to Clean a Cutting Board

A cutting board can be cleaned with a sponge or dishcloth, similar to washing dishes. However, if there are any cuts or bumps in the board, use a scrub brush when washing. Wooden boards should not be soaked or put in dishwasher.

To sanitize the board, make a solution of one part vinegar to 5 parts water. In the sink, pour solution all over the board. Wait 5 minutes. Rinse.

If tools you are using come in contact with raw meat, be sure to thoroughly scrub everything with soap: your hands, all utensils, cutting boards, and the counter, before touching other food. It is best to designate a separate cutting board for meat products to keep the bad bacteria from getting on the vegetables and fruits.

How to Clean a Grater: A grater cleans well with a vigorous swish in

a bowl of water. If you need to scrub the grater, use a brush in the non-cutting direction on the grater so you do not grate the bristles! If you use a drop of soap, rinse well with water. Let grater dry before putting it away.

How to Clean a Knife

Hold the knife by its handle. Wipe the knife on a soapy sponge. Rinse knife with water. Never leave a knife in the sink, especially under water where it might not be seen.

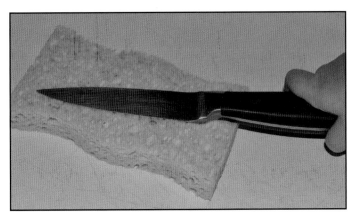

How to Set a Table

4

1. Put a plate on the table near each person's chair.

2. On the left of the plate place a napkin.

3. Put a fork on the napkin with the handle towards edge of the table. Tines of the fork curve up.

3. On the right of the plate place a table knife with the handle towards edge of the table and the sharper side of the blade towards the plate.

4. Place a spoon outside the knife. The bowl of the spoon faces up.

How to Carry and Pass a Knife

To carry a knife, hold it by its handle with the point down. Walk slowly and carefully carrying the knife. To pass the knife to another person, place it on a flat surface and let the other person pick it up.

Refrigerate **leftovers** and eat within 3 days.

BEAN DIP

Yield: 3 cups

Skills learned: opening a can, mixing

Equipment: can opener, liquid measuring cup, large mixing bowl, fork, measuring spoons set, 2 spoons

Ingredients:

1 16-ounce can vegetarian
    refried beans

1 cup salsa

1 Tablespoon prepared yellow
    mustard

Directions:

1. Wash top of can.

2. Open can with can opener (See page 44).

3. Use the spoon to scoop refried beans from can
    into bowl.

4. Measure salsa by using a clean spoon to get it
    from jar into the liquid measuring cup. Add
    salsa to the beans in the bowl.

5. Measure mustard into the tablespoon. Add to
    bowl. If mustard sticks in the tablespoon,
    scoop it out with a spoon.

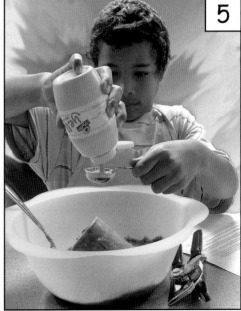

6. Mix with a fork by going halfway around the edge of the bowl and pulling outer ingredients into the middle. Then lift and turn the fork. Turn the bowl half a turn. Repeat. Keep the fork moving strongly and smoothly until all ingredients are combined.

Serving: Place bowl of dip on a large plate. Surround with raw broccoli pieces, baby carrots, tortilla chips, pita chips, or crackers.

This Is a Manual Can Opener:

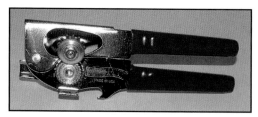

Make sure you have a good-quality easy-to-use hand-held can opener.

Most manually-operated can openers have two hinged arms. On the front of the top arm is a cutting wheel attached to a gear wheel behind it. On the front of the bottom arm is a turning wheel attached to a gear wheel behind it, connected to a butterfly lever on the back. The gear wheels and the turning wheels are toothed. Attached at a right angle to the bottom arm is a distance keeper, which helps maintain the opener in the correct position. When the butterfly lever is turned, the gear wheel on the bottom arm moves the turning wheel, which rotates the can, and simultaneously (at the same time) engages the gear wheel on the top arm to make the cutting wheel turn.

How to Operate a Manual Can Opener:

1. Open handles of the can opener. Keep cutting wheel directly above turning wheel. Hook the cutting wheel over the top lip of the can.

2. Squeeze handles together so the cutting wheel punctures (pierce hole in) the can. Hold handles together firmly.

3. Turn the butterfly lever clockwise to move the cutting wheel around the can until the lid is completely severed.

4. Lift lid off with a fork. The edge is very sharp so be careful. Place lid in sink.

5. After removing contents of can, carefully wash can and lid with a dish brush and water. Recycle can.

6. Brush, wash, and dry can opener wheels.

If using an electric or other style can opener, ask adult for directions.

Q: Who invented the modern can opener with the two wheels? When?

Q: Why is it important to wash the can before discarding?

A: William Lyman in 1870.

A: Food left in cans attracts ants, flies, and animals. The lid should always be completely removed to prevent injury to small animals who enter the can in search of food or shelter.

MASHED BANANA ON RICE CAKES

Yield: 2 servings

Skills learned: peeling banana, mashing

Equipment: 2 plates, masher or fork, measuring spoons set, table knife, spoon

Ingredients:

1 ripe banana

2 teaspoons sesame tahini or nut butter

1 Tablespoon wheat germ

2 rice cakes

Directions:

1. Peel banana (p. 47). Place banana on a plate.

2. Mash banana with fork: A. Hold the fork horizontally with the tines lying on the banana, points of the tines (prongs) pointing upward. Press fork through banana repeatedly to mash. Placing thumb close to the tines makes pressing easier.

2A

2B

OR use the masher: B. Hold masher handle vertically and place the grid on banana. Press down firmly.

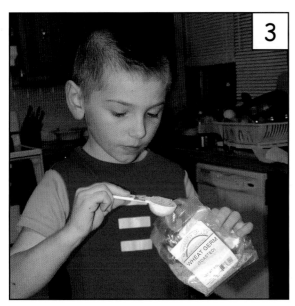

3. Add tahini to banana. Mash tahini into banana. Add wheat germ. Mix.

4. Place the rice cakes on the second plate. Put banana mixture on the rice cakes.

Raisin Banana Rice Cakes

Additional ingredients may be added to the above recipe such as 1 Tablespoon raisins, 1 teaspoon carob powder, and 1 teaspoon shredded coconut. Mix well. (Raisins in #4)

How to Peel a Banana

There are many ways to peel a banana. For example, monkeys hold banana near the stem in one hand with the stem down. Pinch the other end (now on top) of the banana until the end splits into 2 to 4 sections. Pull banana peel down on every side. (If banana has green remaining, it will not peel as easily.) Most people break the stem and pull the peel downwards.

CEREAL WITH FRUIT

Yield: 2 servings (Share with a friend!)

Skills learned: easy cutting, measuring

Equipment: 2 bowls, 1-cup dry measuring cup, cutting board, table knife, liquid measuring cup

Ingredients:

2 cups cereal

1 banana

2 handfuls raisins

1 cup vanilla soymilk

Directions:

1. Measure 1 cup of cereal in dry measuring cup.

2. Pour cereal from cup into a bowl. Repeat measuring; pour into other bowl.

3. Peel banana. Slice banana (p. 49).

4. Put half of the banana slices in each bowl. Rinse hands.

5. Put 1 handful raisins in each bowl.

6. Pour 1 cup soymilk into liquid measuring cup. Use 1/2 cup in each bowl.

How to Slice a Banana with a Table Knife

1. Place peeled banana on cutting board. Hold table knife handle in hand you use for writing. To slice banana, place blade of knife across banana, sharp side down, half inch from the end.

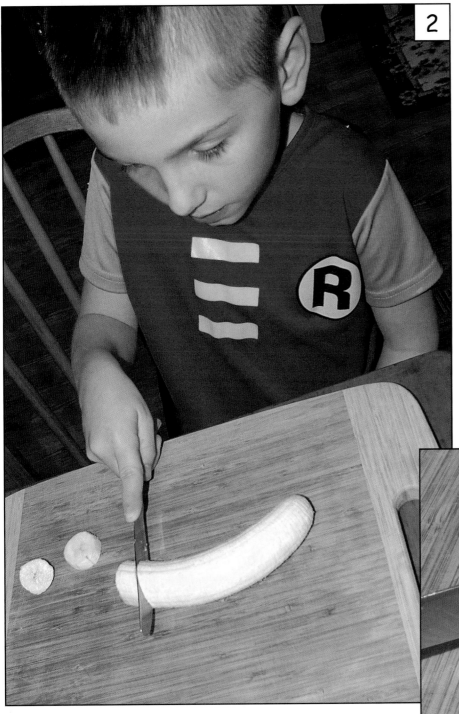

2. Keep the other hand away from the cutting board. Press table knife through banana to make a slice and repeat.

3. When the knife gets close to the end of the banana, turn end on its flat side. End does not roll and does not have to be held. Cut end in half.

AMBROSIA FRUIT SALAD

It is important to have a responsible adult watch child's fingers and technique for the first times cutting food. Discuss knife safety!

Yield: 4 servings

Skill learned: cutting soft food, using a paring knife

Equipment: cutting board, paring knife, 1-quart bowl, liquid measuring cup, 1/4-cup dry measuring cup, big spoon, colander

Ingredients:

1 banana

1/2 cup orange juice

1 pear

8 strawberries

1/4 cup shredded coconut

Directions:

1. Peel and slice banana (p. 51). Place banana slices in the bowl. Pour orange juice over banana slices.

2. Wash pear and remove sticker if there is one. Cut and core pear (p. 52). Place pear in the bowl with the banana. Stir with big spoon.

3. Wash strawberries. Hull and cut strawberries (p. 53). Add berries to bowl.

4. Measure and add coconut to the fruit salad. Stir with the big spoon.

Serving:

Use a big spoon to divide fruit salad among 4 small bowls. Serve with spoons.

How to Slice a Banana Like Famous Chefs Do —

without cutting fingers   (Remember to ask adult to supervise.)

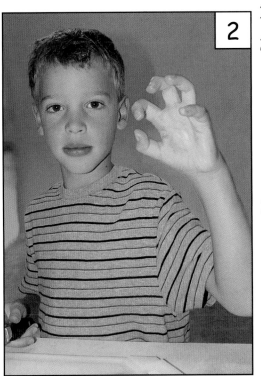

1. Place peeled banana across cutting board.
2. Hold knife handle in one hand with blade across the end of the banana. Make a claw with the other hand to hold the banana at its middle. Keep claw knuckles bent and slightly forward of fingertips.
3. Cut straight down (or slightly tilted away from claw) with knife to make a banana slice. Move knife 1/2 inch towards claw between each cut; slice 1/2-inch-thick rounds. When the knife blade approaches the knuckles, retreat claw to expose more banana.
4. When the remaining banana is too small to hold safely this way, it should be about the size of a strawberry. Turn onto flat edge. Keep other hand away from banana. Slice downward to split it.

How to Cut
and Core a Pear

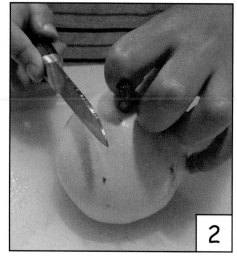

1. Place washed pear on its base (stem up) on cutting board.

2. To cut a pear, think in thirds like tic-tac-toe. Using claw, hold pear next to stem. Place knife blade on the other side of the stem. Press down firmly with knife to cut one third (1/3) off the pear.

3. Put the 1/3 piece flat side down on cutting board. Cut it twice in each direction like tic-tac-toe lines.

4. Put larger (2/3) piece of pear with flat side down on cutting board. Cut in thirds parallel to core. The center third will contain the core.

5. Take the center third and place it on a side so you can see the core. Cut it lengthwise again to remove core and stem.

6. Cut the rest of the pear into small pieces. Remember to keep your claw hand safe!

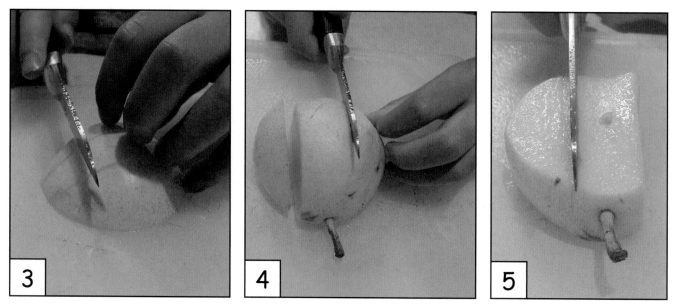

How to Hull and Cut Strawberries

1. To hull (remove green leaves from) the washed strawberries, place the berry on its side on the cutting board. Hold the small end of the berry keeping fingers away from the knife. Carefully slice off the leaves by cutting straight down with knife. (Or leaves may be pinched, twisted, and pulled to remove without using a knife.)

2. Roll berry onto its new flat edge (formerly the top). It should stay in place without being held, so keep other hand away from the knife. Slice downwards to split berry. If desired, place on new bigger flat side and cut again.

STUFFED DATES

Yield: 10 to share with a friend

Equipment: plate, paring knife

Ingredients:

10 dates

10 nuts: almond, Brazil, pecan, or cashew

Directions:

1. Place dates on plate. Put knife on a date lengthwise. Use your non-knife hand to make a bridge with your thumb and index finger over the knife down to the sides of the date to keep it from rolling.
2. Cut half-way through, enough to open the date. Open dates to check for pits. Remove any pits or stems.
3. Put one nut in each date. Close dates. Arrange dates on plate.

ALMOND BUTTER AND CHERRY SANDWICH

A variation on the classic peanut butter and jelly sandwich.

Yield: 1 sandwich

Skills learned:

   spreading,

   cutting bread

Equipment: plate,

   2 table knives,

   Tablespoon

Ingredients:

2 slices whole wheat
   bread

1 Tablespoon black
   cherry jam or other
   all-fruit jam

1 Tablespoon almond
   butter

(For this recipe
   Tablespoons can be
   measured or
   approximate.)

Directions:

1. Place bread on the

   plate. Measure or dip knife blade into the black cherry jam and put it on
   one slice of bread. Spread jam onto the bread by turning the knife on its
   side and sweeping the blade across the slice of bread.

2. Use second knife (or clean tablespoon) to put almond butter on second slice of bread and spread it. Put slices together for sandwich, almond butter against jam.

3. Cut the sandwich in half by holding the sandwich gently against the plate with one hand, keeping fingers away from the knife. Hold knife in the other hand with the point at the far side of the sandwich. Push knife down through the bread and pull toward you.

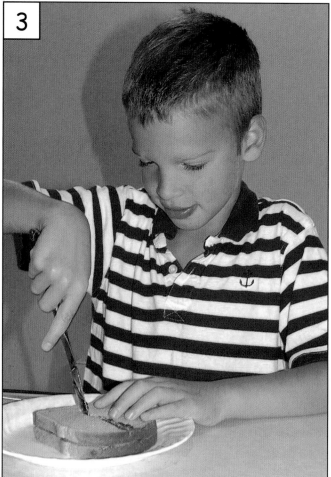

Note: Nut or seed butters can be substituted: coconut, sunflower, sesame, walnut, peanut, cashew, filbert. In natural nut butters, often the oil separates and needs to be stirred back into the butter.

TOFEGG SANDWICH

Yield: 10 small open-faced sandwiches

Skills learned: draining, pressing, and crumbling

Equipment: paring knife, cloth towel, paper towel, large bowl, small spoon, dry measuring cup set, table knife, measuring spoons set, large spoon, cutting board, serrated knife, plate

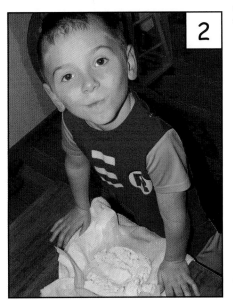

Ingredients:

1 block of firm regular tofu (12 to 16 ounces)

1/4 cup soy mayonnaise

1 Tablespoon prepared yellow mustard

   (Use brown or Dijon mustard if spicy preferred.)

1/2 teaspoon salt, optional ("Optional" means you

   decide whether or not to use it.)

1 small loaf fresh French bread

sprinkle of paprika

Directions:

1. Open and rinse tofu (p. 59).

2. Blot tofu (p. 60). You may press really hard.

3. Place tofu in bowl. Grab a large handful of tofu and make a fist, leaving space for tofu to slide out between your fingers or the end of your fist. Squish all the tofu.

4. Rinse and dry hands.

5. Use a small spoon to scoop mayonnaise into a 1/4-cup dry measuring cup and level top with table knife. Add to the tofu.

6. Measure and add mustard. Measure and add salt. Mix well using a large spoon; the mustard makes it all pale yellow.

7. Slice bread (p. 60) and place slices on a plate.

8. Spoon tofu mixture onto bread and gently press to spread it to the edges. Use approximately 1 tablespoon of the tofu mixture per piece if bread is small, 2 tablespoons if larger.

9. Very gently and slowly, sprinkle top with paprika.

Using Tofu: Opening, Rinsing, and Storing

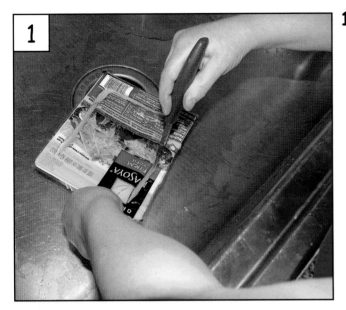

1. **Opening:** For most regular tofu packages, place tofu package in the sink. Puncture one corner with the point of a paring knife. Have the blade facing away from you and slit along the inside edge of the package. Repeat with two more edges. Open top of container like a door and hold it open.

2. **Rinsing:** Place other hand on top of tofu. Keeping tofu over the sink, turn package onto hand to drain water off tofu. Return tofu to container with hand on top. Add water to tofu to rinse it. Keep hand on top, turn and drain again. Set tofu container on counter with open side upwards. Tofu is ready to use.

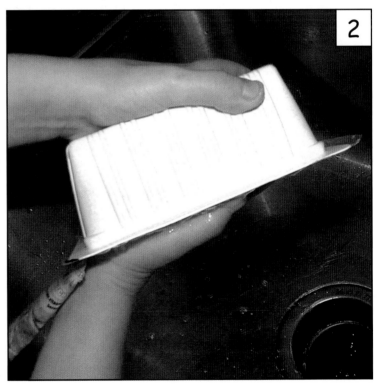

3. **Storing:** If using part of a block of tofu, place remaining tofu in a container. Cover tofu with water. Place lid securely on container. Refrigerate. If water is changed daily, tofu should stay fresh for a week.

Note: Tofu packages have "use by" dates. Always check this when purchasing.

Blotting Tofu

1. Place cloth towel opened on counter. Place paper towel on top of cloth towel. Remove tofu from container. Put block of tofu on paper towel.

2. Wrap tofu in paper towel. Wrap cloth towel around the paper towel.

3. Press on the wrapped tofu to remove excess water. Do not squish tofu unless recipe tells you to press further. Unwrap.

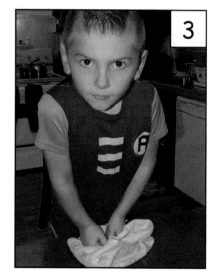

Slicing Bread

1. Place bread on cutting board. Hold handle of serrated knife in hand you use for writing. Place blade of knife across the bread near one end. Hold bread with other hand, keeping fingers away from knife.

2. Use a back-and-forth sawing motion to firmly slice the bread. Repeat to make more slices, moving the other hand safely back on bread before making each slice.

CUCUMBER SANDWICHES

Yield: 2 sandwiches

Skills learned: slicing, mincing

Equipment: 2 plates, measuring spoons set, table knife, bowl, cutting board, chef's knife, peeler, paring knife

Ingredients:

4 slices whole wheat bread

4 Tablespoons soy mayonnaise

12 leaves fresh spearmint

6 sprigs fresh parsley

1 small cucumber

Directions:

1. Place bread on plates. Spread 1 tablespoon mayonnaise with table knife onto each slice of bread.

2. Wash spearmint (mint) and parsley. Pluck mint leaves from stem. Break parsley leaves from stems.

3. Mince mint and parsley (p. 63). Sprinkle mint and parsley onto mayonnaise.

4. Wash cucumber.

5. If it is waxed, peel cucumber (p. 64).

6. Place cucumber on cutting board. With paring knife, cut 1/4 inch off peeled end of cucumber. Slice 1/4-inch-thick rounds to make 10 to 12 slices.

7. Place 5 or 6 cucumber slices on one slice of bread on each plate. Cover with the other slice of bread, mayonnaise side towards cucumber.

8. Cut the sandwich into quarters. Cut in half vertically and horizontally to make square quarters OR cut in half along both diagonals to make triangular quarters.

Note: Two sandwiches may only need half a cucumber depending on size of cucumber and thickness of slices. If the other half is not peeled, it will stay fresh longer in the refrigerator.

Mincing Fresh Herbs

Use for edible decoration on vegetable dishes or in salads.

Skills learned: mincing (very fine chopping), using chef's knife

Equipment: bowl, colander, chef's knife, cutting board

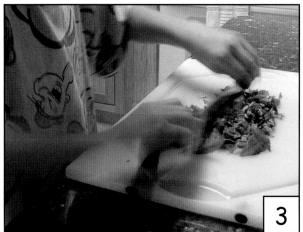

Ingredient: washed parsley leaves, mint leaves, or other herbs

Directions:

1. Hold knife handle in one hand. With the other hand, pinch top of knife near the pointed end. Hold end in place while rocking the handle up and down to cut herbs. Move handle in an arc to continue cutting herbs.

2. Beginning at one edge of the herbs, scrape the knife across the board pulling the herbs with it toward the center. Repeat from each edge until herbs are in a pile.

3. Continue chopping herbs until sufficiently minced.

Peeling a Carrot or Cucumber

1. Hold carrot (or cucumber) against cutting board with one hand, exposing the bottom half of carrot. Hold peeler in the other hand.

2. Place peeler on carrot and push away from you, removing peel.

3. Rotate the carrot each stroke until peel has been removed from the bottom half.

4. Turn carrot around so you are holding the peeled half and repeat process.

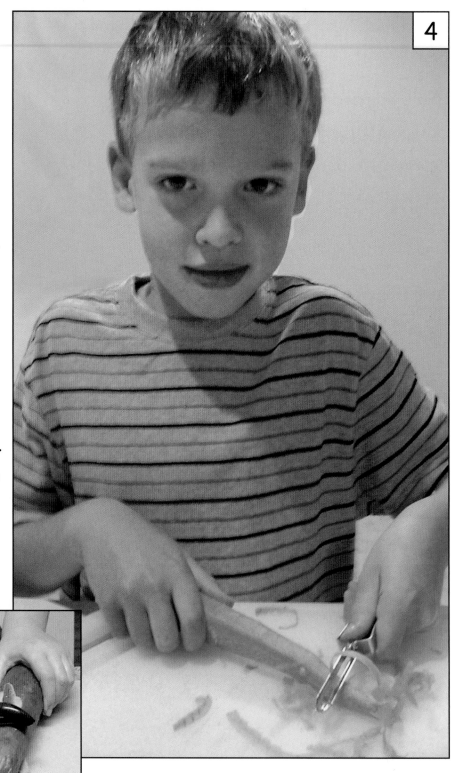

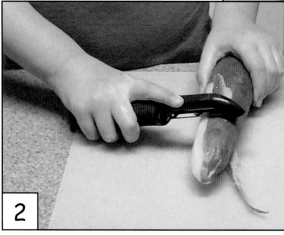

GUACAMOLE

Yield: 1/2 cup

Skills learned: pitting an avocado, juicing a lime or lemon

Equipment: paring knife, cutting board, spoon, fork, plate, medium-large bowl, table knife, lemon squeezer, measuring spoons

Ingredients:

1 Tablespoon lime or lemon juice

1 ripe avocado, Haas variety

1/4 teaspoon chili powder

1/4 teaspoon cumin

1/4 teaspoon salt

Directions:

1. Juice the lime (p. 66). Put 1 tablespoon of lime juice into the medium-large bowl.

2. Wash and pit the avocado (p. 67).

3. Scoop the avocado from its peel using a spoon. Place avocado on a plate. Mash with fork. Put into bowl.

4. Add chili powder. Add cumin. Add salt. Mix well in a mashing style.

Serving: goes well with tortilla chips.

Notes: For a creamier guacamole, add 1 teaspoon soy mayonnaise or soy sour cream. For chunky guacamole, add finely chopped tomato, onion, hot peppers, or cilantro.

How to Juice a Lime or Lemon

1. Wash lime. Roll lime on table, pressing firmly on it to soften.

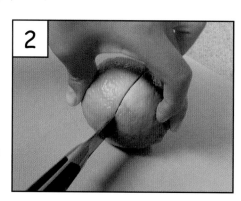

2. Cut lime in half: Place lime on cutting board. Place knife across lime halfway between the ends. With the other hand, bridge over the knife. Cut down in a sawing motion. If lime is hard to cut, tricks include: A. Begin the slice by poking tip of knife to make a slot, then use

knife blade. B. Rotate lime slowly into the knife while pushing down. C. Be above lime to put more pressure on knife.

3. (A) Put lime half cut-side down on spike of juicer. Push straight down with palm of hand while rotating lime. It is easier if you are above the lime to put your weight on it. As it juices, use fingers to press sides of lime towards spike. OR (B) Push a juicing spike into a hand-held lime. Rotate the tool.

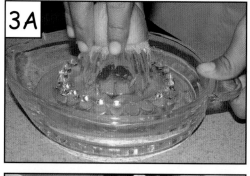

4. Squeeze extra juice by hand.

Note: Limes do not have seeds. Remove seeds from lemon juice before using.

How to Pit an Avocado

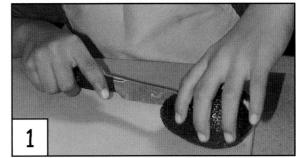

1. Place avocado on cutting board. Place sharp edge of the paring knife blade on the avocado lengthwise. Bridge fingers over knife. Push the knife down to the pit.

2. Slowly rotate the avocado into the knife, keeping the blade against the pit. Remove knife and set aside.

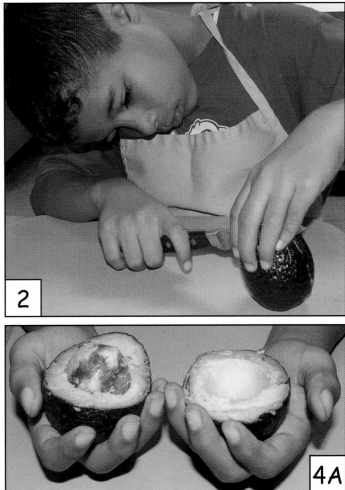

3. Hold avocado in both hands, one on each side of the cut. Twist hands in opposite directions to separate it.

4. If pit remains in one side, cut that side in half again, using the same process as for whole avocado. Hold and twist apart the new quarters in opposite directions. Pit should be easy to pull out.

How Tell If an Avocado Is Ripe

Gently squeeze. Ripe avocado will dent with finger pressure.

CARROT STICKS

Yield: 6 or 8 sticks

Skills learned: peeling carrots, cutting hard rounded objects

Equipment: peeler, paring knife, cutting board, cup

Ingredients:

1 large carrot

water

Directions:

1. Wash carrot under running water and rub off dirt with hands or vegetable scrub brush. Peel carrot.

2. Place carrot on cutting board. Hold middle of the carrot, keeping fingers away from knife. To trim end off carrot, touch the point of the knife to the cutting board and rock knife down through carrot. Turn other end toward knife, hold middle, and trim.

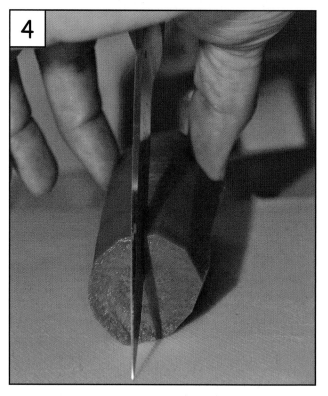

3. Hold one end of the carrot. Cut carrot across at the middle.

4. Place knife blade lengthwise on top of a carrot piece. Make a bridge with your thumb and index finger over the knife down to the sides of the carrot. Hold carrot firmly against the cutting board. Tip knife point onto cutting board. Cut carrot from one end to the other by pushing knife down.

5. When you have cut down enough that the knife holds the carrot from rolling, press bridge down. Repeat process until you have sliced each piece once lengthwise.

6. Place flat side of each piece on cutting board and slice lengthwise again to make quarters. Depending on the size of the carrot, you might opt to only do this step to the top parts of the carrot.

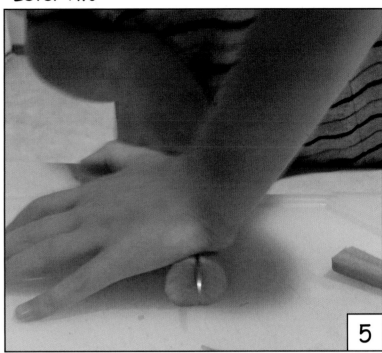

5

7. Place carrot sticks in a cup that is taller than the length of the longest sticks. Cover sticks with water and refrigerate for a few hours. Sticks can be eaten immediately after cutting, but they taste better if soaked in water.

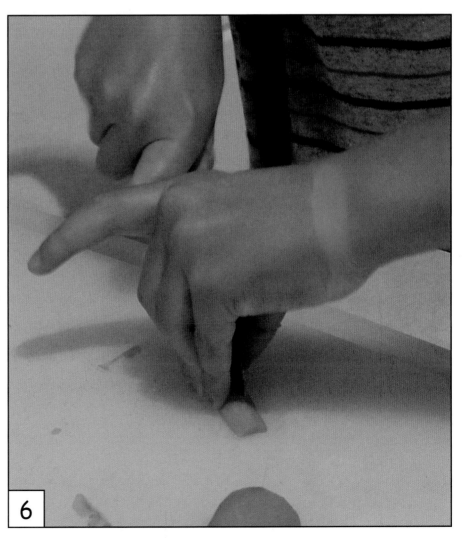

6

DELUXE SALAD

Yield: 6 servings

Skills learned: grating, dicing

Equipment: large bowl, colander, peeler, grater, cutting board, paring knife, serrated knife, can opener

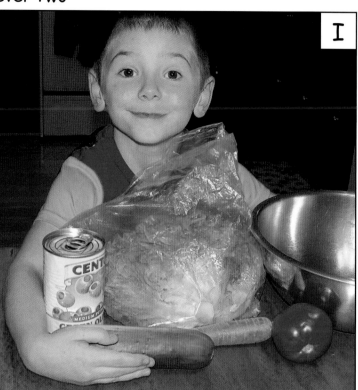

Ingredients:

4 lettuce leaves, any leafy variety

1 carrot

1 cucumber

1 large tomato

1 15-ounce can pitted olives, black or green

Directions:

1. Wash lettuce. Wash carrot. Wash cucumber. Wash tomato. Wash top of olives can.

2. Shake or spin water off lettuce (p. 72). Rip lettuce into bowl.

3. Peel carrot. Grate carrot (p. 73). If grater is not available,

continue peeling carrot into lots of carrot strips. Put carrot in bowl.

4. If cucumber is waxed, peel cucumber. Place cucumber on cutting board. Use the paring knife to cut cucumber into rounds. Cut the rounds into bite-sized pieces. Add cucumber to the bowl.

5. Place tomato on cutting board on its flattest side (usually stem area). Cut tomato in half using serrated knife in a careful sawing motion. Place each half flat side down and continue cutting until pieces are bite-sized. Remove core. Add tomato to bowl.

6. Mix salad with your hands.

7. Keep olives can near the sink. Use can opener to remove top. Put your hand on top of the can to hold back the olives and drain olive brine into sink. Top the salad with olives.

Note: Additional items may be used or substituted such as:
1 15-ounce can black beans (drained),
1 avocado (peeled, pitted, and chopped),
1/4 cup raisins,
5 leaves spinach (washed and ripped),
1/4 cup nuts.

How to Spin Salad Leaves

Spinning is recommended when making more than one serving of salad. It uses centrifugal force to remove water from leaves.

If using a salad spinner:

1. Put spinner in sink. Place washed lettuce in spinner basket. Securely attach lid.
2. Holding spinner, crank the handle quickly.
3. Let spinner stop. Open. Remove lettuce.

If using a pillowcase:

1. Place washed lettuce in small pillowcase. Twist open end of pillowcase 3 times, or tie knot, or zip it up.
2. Go outside to an open space. Grab pillowcase tightly at the twist or knot, holding it so pillowcase will not touch the ground.
3. Spin pillowcase really fast by spinning yourself around and around OR circling your arm next to your body or over your head.
4. Return to the kitchen. Open pillowcase. Remove lettuce.

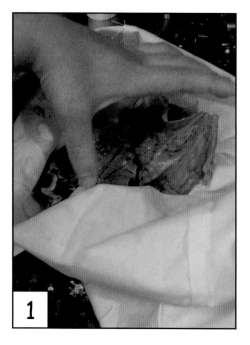

Grated Carrot

Equipment: vegetable scrub brush, peeler, paring knife, cutting board, grater, plate

Ingredient: 1 large carrot

Directions:

1. Wash carrot with vegetable scrub brush under running water.

2. Peel carrot.

3. Cut off bottom end. Leave top end on to hold while grating.

4. Hold grater (2 types shown) on plate with one hand. Hold top (larger end) of carrot with other hand. Press bottom (smaller) end of carrot to the grater, keeping fingers away from grater holes. In A, scrape carrot against the grater in firm downward (vertical) motions, In B, use sideways (horizontal) motions. Stop grating before fingers get close to the grating surface.

APPLE MUESLI

Yield: 2 servings

Skills learned: peeling apples, grating apples

Equipment: large bowl, dry measuring cups, liquid measuring cup, measuring spoons set, table knife, peeler, grater, plate, spoon

Ingredients:

1/2 cup quick oats

1/4 cup raisins

1 Tablespoon shredded coconut, optional

1 cup soymilk or water

1 large apple, yellow delicious preferred

1/4 teaspoon cinnamon, optional

Directions:

1. Place oats in bowl. Add raisins. Add coconut.

2. Add soymilk. Mix.

3. Wash apple. Peel apple (p. 75) and grate it (p. 77). Place apple in the bowl. Mix.

4. Sprinkle cinnamon on top.

Serving: Put in 2 bowls. Share with a friend.

2

How to Peel an Apple, Basic Method

An apple can be peeled somewhat like a carrot.

1. Hold handle of peeler in the hand you use to write. Hold apple in opposite hand.

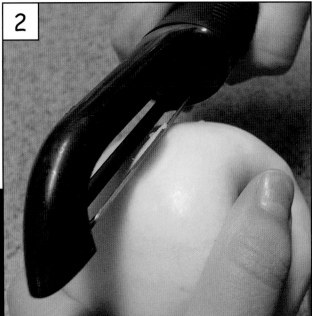

2. Place peeler at the top of the apple and push into the apple until peeler begins to cut apple. Maintaining pressure on apple, push down and away to remove peel.

3. Turn apple slightly and repeat until apple is completely peeled. You will remove many strips of peel.

How to Peel an Apple, Advanced Method

1. Hold handle of the peeler in one hand and apple in opposite hand.

2. Place peeler on an angle at the top of the apple. Keep fingers of peeler hand on the handle while thumb presses on the apple. Pull into the apple until peeler begins to cut apple.

3. Hold the peeler and turn the apple into the peeler. The cutting blade should stay on the apple. Use thumb to guide peeler, stepping thumb around, while turning apple with other hand. Gradually lower the peeler to follow peeled edge.

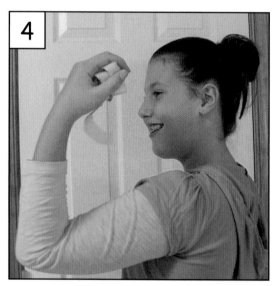

4. Practice frequently; when you get it in one continuous spiral, throw peel over the left shoulder and make a wish.

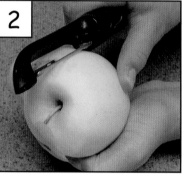

5. Look at the peel on the floor and interpret meaning before putting peel in the compost.

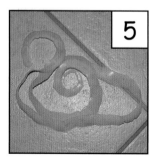

How to Grate an Apple

1. With one hand, hold grater firmly on a plate or bowl. Using the other hand, put thumb and fingers on opposite ends of the apple.

2. Rub sides of apple against the grater, back and forth or up and down depending on style of grater, keeping fingers away from sharp grater blades. As you approach the core, rotate apple and continue grating.

Stop grating when apple is down to the core or fingers can no longer be kept safely away from the grater blades.

Level Three:
Using Stove and Oven

Safety and Cleanup

Before starting to cook, have a safety plan and an emergency plan.
Brainstorm with an adult emergency scenarios prior to using any heat source.
Know when and how to: smother a fire, use a fire extinguisher, and exit.

Stove and Oven Safety

1. Keep hands away from burners, especially gas flames.

2. Hold pot handle to keep pot from slipping when stirring. Keep handles of pots away from stove edges so pots will not accidentally be bumped and spill. Also handles should not be over another burner. Do not reach across a hot burner or pot.

3. When checking pot, lift knob towards you, tilting lid to shield you from escaping steam.

4. Put stirring spoon on a spoon rest or saucer so it does not get the stove dirty. Use heat resistant spoons.

5. Always use thick, dry pot holders or oven mitts when touching anything hot on the stove, in the oven, in the microwave, or under the broiler.

6. When a pot or pan is heavy, ask an adult to move it for you.

7. Always turn off stove and oven when done. Remember, it will still be hot.

8. Keep everything off the stove, except pots that are cooking or just finished cooking. Oven mitts, paper, paper towels, and plastic utensils can all melt or catch on fire. Keep this book away from the stove!

9. Keep electrical cords away from the stove. Electrical cords must not be near water nor heat.

10. Some stoves and ovens may heat at slightly different temperatures, which may require adjustments in cooking times.

11. Knobs may be in various locations: be careful reaching over stove if knobs are at the back.

12. Always watch pot come to boil. Stay in the kitchen when cooking on stove.

How to Check If Pot Is Big Enough: Add all amounts of ingredients and measure that volume of water into the pot. It should be less than 3/4 full. Dump out the water and use the actual ingredients. Use a burner that is equal to or slightly smaller than the pot's diameter.

Using a Timer and Clock

Set the timer for the cooking time. This can be done by using a touch pad on a digital timer OR by turning the knob on a dial timer to point at the required time. As a backup,

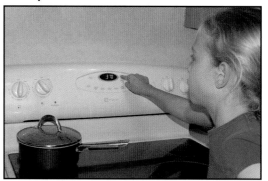

look at a clock or watch. Write down the current time and add the cooking time to determine when it will be done. Remember: 60 minutes in an hour.

Microwave Ovens: It is controversial whether using a microwave oven is healthful. Microwaves are common for heating food. When cooking food, it often tastes better to use conventional stove and oven methods. Some foods commonly cooked with oil, such as mushrooms and onions, can be cooked in the microwave without oil. If using a microwave, consult the microwave's directions for cooking times. This book is not designed for microwave use, but there is one basic microwave recipe included (Baked Potatoes).

2A How to Clean Pots and Pans

1. Place pot in sink. If food is stuck to pot, put water in pot and allow to soak a few minutes to loosen food.
2. Ask if the pot has a surface that would scratch easily. If so, wash with a soapy sponge (A).

   For pots that don't scratch, use a scouring pad (B).
3. Rinse.
4. Set pot in dish-draining rack to dry.

How to Clean a Stove or Oven

Let everything cool before wiping any spills. Get a sponge or cloth wet and wring it out well. Wipe the stove or oven. Wipe up a spill before the next use burns it on and makes it difficult to clean. Rinse and wring sponge. Major cleaning of a stove or oven should be done by an adult.

SUCCOTASH

Yield: 4 servings

Skills learned: boiling, testing doneness, using stove

Equipment: scissors, medium pot with lid, 2-cup liquid measuring cup, 2 twist ties, timer, paring knife, cutting board

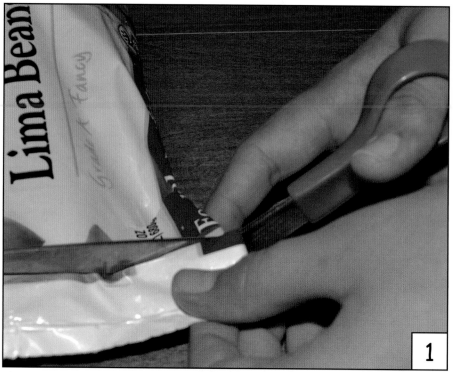

Ingredients:

2 cups frozen lima beans

2 cups frozen cut corn

1 cup water

Directions:

1. Place bag of frozen lima beans on counter, away from the edge. Cut off one end with scissors.

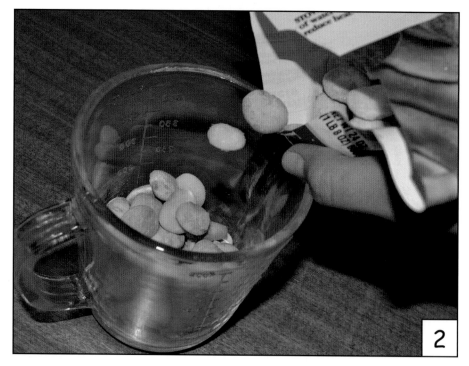

2. Carefully lift bag of limas so the open end is over the measuring cup. Slowly pour limas to measure. Place limas in pot. If some limas remain in the bag, close the end of bag with a twist tie and return it to the freezer.

3. Repeat steps 1 and 2 for corn.

4. Measure and add water to pot.

5. Place pot on burner. Turn burner to high heat. **Watch pot as it comes to boil** (when water bubbles).

6. Reduce heat to medium-low. Cover pot with lid. Set timer and cook for 10 minutes; **stay in the kitchen while it cooks**. If lots of steam escapes the lid, lower the heat.

7. Carefully remove lid, lift knob towards you, tilting lid to shield you from escaping steam. Pierce one lima with a paring knife and remove it. Replace lid. Place lima on cutting board. Cut in half. A done lima will be the same green and soft all the way through. If not done, cook for 2 more minutes.

8. Turn off burner. Remove pot from heat and set on a heat-resistant surface.

Serving: Use slotted serving spoon.

Notes: A large 2-cup liquid measure is easier to use than dry measures for this recipe.

Frozen food takes longer to come to boil than fresh vegetables.

As you get familiar with cooking, the lima can be tested for doneness by placing in cold water, then eating.

STEAMED ASPARAGUS

Yield: 4 servings

Skills learned: breaking asparagus stems, washing sandy vegetable

Equipment: large bowl, colander, medium pot with lid, liquid measuring cup, fork

Ingredients:

1 bunch asparagus

1 cup water

Always watch a pot on high heat. Stay in the kitchen when you are cooking on the stove. Remember this for future recipes.

Directions:

1. Remove rubber band (if there is one) from asparagus. Take each spear of asparagus in your two hands and snap off lower, thick end and discard it. Place asparagus spears in a large bowl.

2. Place bowl in the sink and fill with water. Wash asparagus by swishing it vigorously in the water. Place asparagus in colander. Look at the bowl of water while draining the water into the sink. If sand is in the bottom of the bowl, wash asparagus again. Repeat until water is clean. Leave colander of asparagus draining into the sink.

3. Put 1 cup water into the pot. Put asparagus into the pot with spears level or the tips tilted up.

4. Put pot on burner. Turn burner to high heat. Bring to boil.

5. Reduce heat to low. Put lid on pot. Set timer and cook for 10 minutes.

6. Carefully open lid, lift knob towards you, tilting lid to shield you from escaping steam. Pierce asparagus with a fork to determine if it is tender (fork slides in easily). If not tender, cook for 2 more minutes.

7. Turn off burner. Remove pot from heat onto a heat-resistant surface.

Serving: Use tongs to put asparagus on plate.

STEAMED BROCCOLI

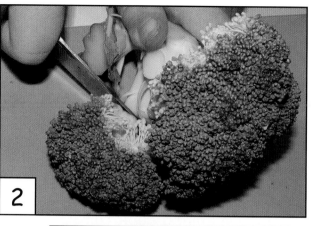

Yield: 4 servings

Skills learned: the basics for steaming most vegetables: wash, chop, cook.

Equipment: large bowl, cutting board, paring knife, medium pot with lid, steamer basket (optional), liquid measuring cup

Ingredients:

1 large broccoli crown

2 cups water

Directions:

1. Place large bowl in sink and fill with water. Wash broccoli by swishing it in water. Shake off excess water.

2. Place broccoli on its side on the cutting board. Hold the stem; cut flowerets from stem, cutting down away from you. Rotate broccoli as needed. Chop the stem into bite-sized pieces.

3. Put water in pot. Open steamer basket in pot (if using one). Add broccoli.

4. Place pot on burner. Turn burner to high heat. Bring to boil.

5. Reduce heat to low. Cover with lid. Cook for 8 minutes. (Cook less time if you prefer firm, more if you prefer soft.)

6. Turn off burner. Remove pot from heat and place on a heat-resistant surface

Serving: Use a slotted serving spoon or tongs.

Note: Water leaches vitamins from vegetables, but makes good vegetable stock for stews. A steamer basket helps vegetables keep vitamins.

OATMEAL

Yield: 3 servings

Skill learned: stir hot item

Equipment: small pot with lid, 1-cup dry measuring cup, liquid measuring cup, table knife, large spoon

Ingredients:

1 cup quick oats

2 cups water

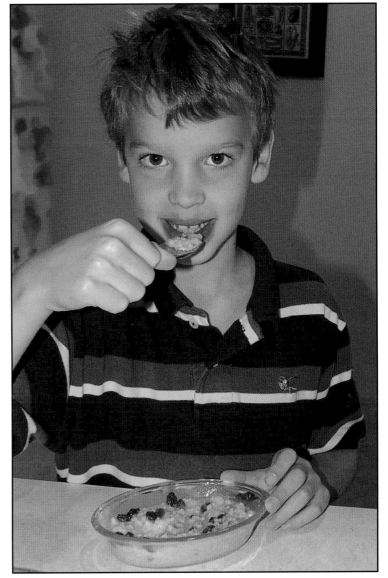

Directions:

1. Measure oats and set aside.
2. Measure water and pour into small pot. Place pot on burner. Turn burner to high heat. Bring to boil.
3. Add oats to pot. Stir once around pot. Place lid on pot.
4. Turn off burner. Allow pot of oatmeal to sit on burner for 5 minutes.

Serving: Divide oatmeal into 3 small bowls. Serve with your favorite additions such as soymilk, maple syrup, brown sugar, chopped dates, raisins, blueberries, ground flaxseed, sliced banana, or chopped apple. Eat with small spoons when oatmeal has cooled to desired temperature. It will thicken as it cools.

Note: For thinner oatmeal, use more water.

BROWN RICE

Yield: 6 servings

Skills learned: precise dry and wet measuring, washing grain, simmering

Equipment: medium pot with lid, liquid measuring cup, 1-cup dry measuring cup, medium-sized strainer

Ingredients:

1 cup brown rice

2 1/2 cups water

Directions:

1. Put 1-cup size dry measuring cup on the counter. Pour rice into cup until it almost reaches the top. Level the top of the rice with fingers. Remove or add rice as needed until rice is even with top of cup.

2. Put rice in strainer. Hold strainer and move under running water for 30 seconds; count seconds by saying, "One- I'm washing rice, two- I'm washing rice, three- (go to 30)." Dump rice into pot.

3. Measure 2 1/2 cups of water by first filling the water to the 2-cup line of a 2-cup liquid measure (or a one-cup measure twice). Put water into pot with the rice. Measure an additional 1/2 cup of water and add to pot.

4. Place pot on burner. Watch pot until water comes to a boil.

5. Reduce heat to low. Let simmer (small bubbles breaking surface). Place lid on pot. Set timer. Cook rice for 45 minutes or until rice absorbs all the water. Turn off burner. Remove pot from heat.

6. Let rice stand 10 minutes before serving.

Notes: Holes of strainer should be small enough that the rice will not drop through the holes.

Check directions on package. Some varieties of brown rice require different amounts of water or cooking time. Elevation, temperature of surroundings, and type of stove all affect cooking time. White rice takes only about 15 minutes to cook.

Short-grain rice is stickier than long-grain rice.

RUSTIC MASHED POTATOES

Yield: 3 servings

Skills learned: scrubbing potatoes, mashing with a masher

Equipment: large bowl, vegetable scrub brush, medium pot with lid, colander, masher, liquid measuring cup, measuring spoons set, table knife, fork, large spoon

Ingredients:

6 small new white potatoes

2 cups water

1/4 cup unsweetened plain soymilk

1 Tablespoon soy margarine

1/2 teaspoon salt, optional

Directions:

1. Put potatoes in large bowl in the sink. Fill bowl with water. Scrub potatoes under water, which prevents splattering the dirt. Rinse potatoes.

2. Place potatoes in the pot. Add 2 cups water.

3. Place pot on burner. Set burner to high heat. Bring to boil.

4. Reduce heat to medium-low. Place lid on pot. If steam escapes, reduce heat. Set timer and continue cooking for 30 minutes.

5. Carefully remove lid, tilting its knob towards you so steam escapes away from you. Poke largest potato with a fork; be sure to puncture into potato to feel the center. If the potato is soft, turn off burner. If the potato is still hard in the center, replace lid and cook 5 more minutes. Repeat this step if necessary.

6. Turn off burner. Remove lid. Allow potatoes to cool for 2 minutes. Place colander in sink. Drain potatoes into colander.

7. Place pot on a sturdy heat-resistant low work surface. Return potatoes to the pot.

8. Mash with potato masher by pressing firmly downward on the handle. Move masher to another part of the pot, press, and repeat until potatoes are all mashed.

9. Add the soymilk. Add margarine and salt. Mix well.

Notes: Peeling potatoes is optional as long as the dirt has been scrubbed off. Many vitamins are just under the skin. Leaving the skin on the potatoes gives mashed potatoes healthy rustic brown flecks. Keeping the lid on the pot while cooking saves energy and allows the potatoes to cook faster. Only remove lid when specified. For thick mashed potatoes, use less soymilk; for thinner, use more soymilk.

MINTED PEAS

Yield: 2 1/2 cups

Equipment: dry measuring cups, strainer, small pot with lid, liquid measuring cup, wooden spoon, cutting board, chef's knife

Ingredients:

1 cup green split peas

2 1/4 cups water

1/2 cup fresh spearmint leaves (packed down)

Directions:*

*By now you know to measure the ingredients, place pot on burner, boil water on high heat, carefully remove lid, set the timer, and turn off the burner. These steps will not be in directions.

1. Put split peas in strainer. Rinse under running water. Put split peas in pot.

2. Put water in pot. Bring water to a boil.

3. Reduce heat to low. Adjust to keep at a gentle simmer. **Caution:** If heat is too high, ingredients will rise and spill. After the bubbles settle, place lid on pot. Cook for 45 minutes until peas are very soft. Stir peas to puree.

4. (Do while peas cook on low.) Pick spearmint. Wash mint. Mince mint. Stir into peas.

Serving: Tastes great warm or cold. Cold Minted Peas solidify; serve using a scoop.

FRUIT JELL

Yield: 2 cups

Skill learned: stirring liquid while heating

Equipment: medium pot with lid, large wooden flat-ended spoon, table knife, liquid measuring cup, 1/2-cup dry measuring cup

Ingredients:

2 cups fruit juice such as berry, apple, or grape

1/4 cup instant tapioca granules

Directions:

1. Put juice in a medium pot. Add tapioca. Stir. Let stand 10 minutes.

2. On medium heat stir with flat-ended spoon while scraping bottom of pot — a slow figure-8 pattern works well. Bring to a ROLLING BOIL, which does not stop bubbling as you stir. This will take about 10 minutes. Keep your face away from the steam.

3. Leave for one hour or until pot is not warm to touch. Refrigerate overnight.

Optional: Jell may be poured carefully into a serving dish while hot.

Note: Orange juice is not good for this recipe because it thickens like pulp.

BAKED POTATOES

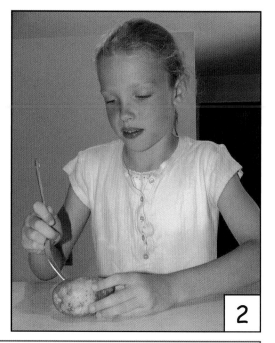

Yield: one potato per person

Skill learned: stabbing potatoes, using oven, using microwave oven

Equipment: large bowl, vegetable scrub brush, fork or paring knife, oven mitts, plate

Ingredients:

1 potato per person, large white russet baking potato preferred

Directions:

1. Scrub potato(es).

> If you must leave the kitchen while using oven, set a portable timer and take it with you.

2. Hold potato firmly against counter with one hand. In part of the potato not too close to your hand, carefully stab each potato twice with a fork or the point of a paring knife. Stabbing potatoes allows steam to escape while baking, otherwise potato may explode.

Microwave Oven:

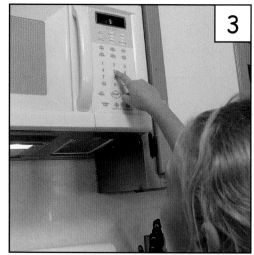

3. Place potato(es) in the microwave. Set timer for 5 minutes or as suggested on microwave directions timing guide. It will take more time for more potatoes.

4. When timer dings, hold potato steady wearing oven mitts and stab potato through the center. If done, inside is soft.

5. If it is not done, turn potato over. Close oven and continue baking another minute or two before rechecking. Repeat this step if necessary.

6. Using oven mitt, carefully remove potato and place on a plate.

Standard Oven:

3. Place potato(es) in the oven. Bake at 375 degrees Fahrenheit (°F) for 45 minutes to 1 hour depending on potato size. (Big potatoes take longer to bake than small potatoes.)

4. When baking time has elapsed, open the door to the oven, keeping your face and limbs away from the hot air escaping the door. Using two oven mitts, slide the rack of potatoes partially out towards you. Stab potato once pressing fork or knife all the way to the center to check if it is done. A done potato will be soft on the inside.

5. If it is not done, slide rack in, close oven, and continue baking a few minutes before rechecking. Repeat this step if necessary.

6. Turn off oven. Using oven mitts, carefully remove potato(es) and place on a plate.

Serving: Allow potato to cool enough to touch. Cut potato open with knife or fork. If desired, add margarine, seasonings, or toppings such as broccoli or baked beans.

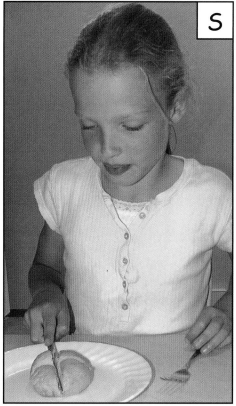

Note: White potatoes may be placed directly on the baking rack. To bake sweet potatoes, which ooze syrup, use a baking sheet, pan, or aluminum foil to keep from making a big mess.

PITA PIZZA

Yield: one personal pizza

Equipment: paring knife, paper towel, cloth towel, bowl, liquid measuring cup, spoon, cutting board, table knife, baking sheet, oven mitts, lifting spatula, dry 1/4-cup measure, teaspoon

Original Olive

Ingredients:

1/4 pound (3/4 cup or 4 ounces) firm
    regular tofu

1/3 cup pasta sauce

1 pita bread (8-inch diameter)

4 pitted olives

Directions:

1. Open and rinse tofu. Blot and press
    tofu until it squishes.

2. Place tofu in bowl. Crumble tofu by
    squeezing with hands. Rinse hands.

3. Preheat oven to 375°F.

4. Place pita flat on baking sheet or concave (bowl-shaped) side up.

5. Mix pasta sauce with tofu. Put tofu sauce on pita.

6. Slice olives on cutting board. Top pizza with olives.

7. Using oven mitts, put baking sheet in oven. Bake 12 minutes. Turn off oven.

8. Using oven mitts, remove baking sheet from oven and place on a heat-
    resistant surface. If preferred, slide out oven rack (use mitts) and use
    lifting spatula to remove pizza and place on a plate.

Spinach Hummus Pizza

1 pita bread

1/4 cup pasta sauce

3 spinach leaves

1/4 cup hummus (a spread/dip made from chickpeas)

1. Preheat oven to 375°F. Place pita flat on baking sheet or concave side up.

2. Spread sauce on pita with table knife.

3. Wash spinach and shake off excess water. Rip leaves from stalks. Arrange spinach on sauce. Spread hummus on spinach.

4. Bake for 12 minutes. Turn off oven. Remember to use the oven mitts!

Making Pizzas:

Emily layers Spinach Hummus Pizza while Charlie works on Bean Corn. Original Olive is ready to bake.

Bean Corn Pizza

1 pita bread

1/4 cup pasta sauce

1/4 cup refried beans

2 teaspoons frozen cut corn

1. Preheat oven to 375°F. Place pita on baking sheet.
2. Put pasta sauce into bowl. Add beans. Mix well. Use a spoon to put bean sauce on pita; spread it with back of spoon.
3. Top with corn. Press corn into bean sauce.
4. Bake for 12 minutes. Turn off oven.

Pita Pizzas ready to eat.
Back left: Original Olive
Right: Spinach Hummus
Front: Variable Topping

Variable Topping Pizza

1 pita bread

1/4 cup pasta sauce

1/4 cup of any of the following: mushrooms, tomato slices, cooked sweet potato slices, steamed & drained vegetables, sliced artichoke hearts, sliced peppers, cooked beans, or other toppings. Use your own ideas.

1. Preheat oven to 375°F. Place pita on baking sheet.
2. Spread sauce on pita.
3. Distribute toppings evenly on sauce.
4. Bake for 12 minutes. Turn off oven.

SUSHI

Yield: 6 servings

Equipment: dry measuring cups set, measuring spoons set, cutting board, paring knife, peeler, spoon, grater, plate, sushi mat, hand towel, small bowl, serrated knife

Ingredients:

6 pieces nori (seaweed paper)

2 cups cooked Brown Rice

water

soy sauce

Pick two of the following:

1 avocado, sliced

1 cucumber, matchstick-
    sliced (p. 101)

12 strips roasted pepper,
    1/4-inch wide

1 carrot, peeled and grated

(For 12-serving sushi party use all 4 filling options; double nori and rice.)

Directions:

1. Place bamboo sushi rolling mat on counter with sticks horizontally. Place one piece nori on mat, groovy side up.

2. Distribute 1/3 cup rice evenly on the bottom half of nori. Keep rice 1/2-inch from edges.

3. Add choice of the other ingredients, not to exceed 1/4 cup, in a line on top of the rice. Rinse and dry hands. Put some water in small bowl.

4. Begin rolling nori and mat away from you. Use fingertips to push leading nori edge over, and tuck under filling.

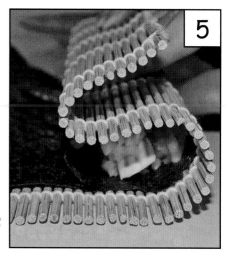

5. Use the mat to roll the nori, gently squeezing as you go. Make the edge of the mat fall back towards you as the nori rolls onto itself.

6. When you arrive at the nori-only edge, dip fingertips into bowl of water. Wipe your fingers along the final edge of the nori. Press edge to sushi roll to seal it. Dry hands.

7. Roll the mat completely around the sushi; squeeze it to make a firm roll. Unwrap the mat from the sushi.

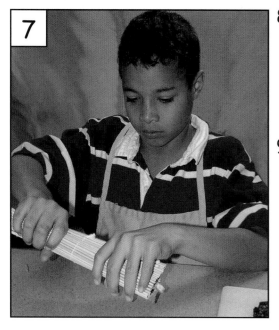

8. Place sushi roll on a cutting board and slice into 6 bite-sized pieces, approximately 1-inch wide, using a very sharp serrated knife.

9. Repeat process for remaining ingredients to make 5 more rolls. Clean serrated knife between cutting rolls.

Serving: Place sushi on a plate. Put soy sauce in small bowl for dipping.

Cucumber Matchsticks

1. Wash and peel cucumber.
2. Place cucumber on cutting board. Slice off ends with paring knife. Slice cucumber in half lengthwise.
3. Cut cucumber crosswise into lengths that equal a wooden matchstick.
4. Cut cucumber into matchstick-width pieces.

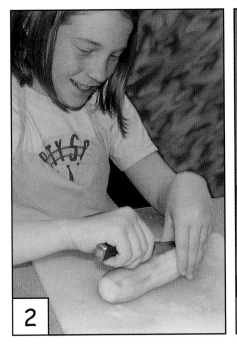

2

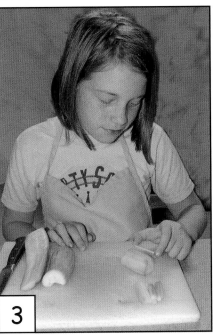

3

4

101

BAKED TOFU SANDWICH

Yield: 4 sandwiches

Equipment: measuring spoons set, 8-inch square pan, fork, cutting board, ruler, serrated knife, paper towel, cloth towel, pillowcase or salad spinner, oven mitts, lifting spatula, plate, table knife.

Ingredients:

3 Tablespoons soy sauce

1 Tablespoon olive oil

1 teaspoon curry powder

1/2 teaspoon mixed dried herbs

1 block (approximately 1 pound) tofu, regular firm or extra firm

1 tomato

4 small lettuce leaves

8 slices whole grain bread

Choose soy mayonnaise, salsa, ketchup, or mustard - 2 teaspoons per slice of bread

Directions:

1. Preheat oven to 375°F. Put soy sauce into baking pan. Add oil. Add curry powder (measured over plate). Crush in herbs by rubbing between hands above the pan. Tilt pan and mix with fork.

2. Open and drain tofu. Place tofu on cutting board. Use serrated knife to cut tofu into 6 even slices, between 1/2-inch and 3/4-inch thick. (You may want to measure and draw a cutting plan on paper.) Blot tofu with towels.

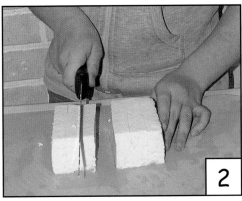

3. Place tofu slices into baking pan. Turn tofu over so marinade is on both sides. Rinse hands.

4. Bake for 20 to 30 minutes or until browned and beginning to dry. (Check in 20 minutes.)

5. While tofu is baking, wash tomatoes and lettuce. Spin dry the lettuce. Use serrated knife and cutting board to slice tomato into at least 4 slices.

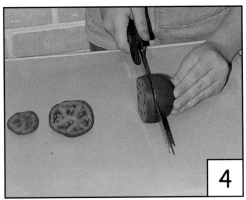

6. Place two slices of bread on plate. Spread with condiment of choice. Rip a lettuce leaf in half. Place half a lettuce leaf on each slice of bread. Put a slice of tomato on one side of the lettuce.

7. When tofu has finished baking, use oven mitts to remove pan from oven and place pan on heat-resistant surface. Turn off oven. Keep one oven mitt on your hand for securing pan while doing the next step.

8. Slice 2 pieces of tofu in half lengthwise. Use lifting spatula to remove tofu from pan. Put one and a half slices of tofu on the tomato. Cover with the other slice of bread, lettuce side down. Repeat process to make remaining 3 sandwiches.

GINGERBREAD COOKIES

Yield: one dozen gingerbread men, approximately 3 1/4-inch tall

Skill learned: using a rolling pin and cookie cutter

Equipment: 2 mixing bowls, dry measuring cup set, liquid measuring cup, measuring spoons set, big spoon, table knife, plate, whisk, plastic wrap, rolling pin, ruler, cookie cutter, baking sheet, lifting spatula, cooling rack

Ingredients:

Dry ingredients:

1 cup whole wheat pastry flour

3/4 cup whole wheat bread flour

   (can be measured as 1/2 + 1/4)

1/4 cup raw cane sugar or other dry sugar

1 teaspoon ground ginger

1/2 teaspoon salt

1/4 teaspoon nutmeg

1/4 teaspoon baking soda

Wet ingredients:

1/4 cup vegetable oil

1/4 cup molasses

2 Tablespoons water

*As you advance, directions may be given for a group of ingredients instead of each item individually. Recipes will not tell when to use oven mitts, turn off oven, or set hot pan on heat-resistant surface. Adult recipe books assume you will know to do this.

Decorations:

Sunflower seeds, chocolate chips, and/or raisins

Directions:*

1. Be very precise when measuring ingredients for baking. Place all dry ingredients in a large mixing bowl. Mix.

2. Place all wet ingredients in the second mixing bowl—do in the order listed. Mix vigorously with a whisk until emulsified (combine 2 liquids until 1 is suspended in other).

3. Pour the wet ingredients into the dry ingredients' bowl. Mix; begin with spoon; use hands as mixture gets stiff. Form into one ball in bowl. If ball is crumbly, wet hands to form ball. Rinse hands.

4. Take one piece of plastic wrap, approximately 12 inches square, and place it on counter. Put ball of dough on plastic wrap. Place another 12-inch square of plastic wrap on top of the dough. (Cut plastic wrap on the box edge carefully or use scissors.)

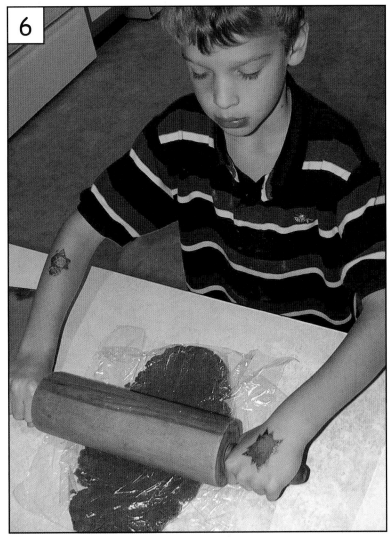

5. Preheat oven to 375°F.

6. With a rolling pin, roll the dough to 1/4 inch thick; roll → horizontally, ↑ vertically, and ↗ diagonally.

7. Remove top sheet of plastic wrap and set aside. Cut with a cookie cutter, sharp side down. Repeat and position cutter close to previous cookies to get the most cookies.

8. Pull away excess dough from cookies. Use lifting spatula to put cookies on an ungreased baking sheet. Make dough scraps into a new ball, reroll, and cut to make additional cookies.

9. Bake cookies for 10 to 12 minutes. Cookies will be soft and may have lightly browned edges when done. Carefully move cookies individually with lifting spatula from baking sheet to cooling rack.

10. Decorate cookies while warm. Press sunflower seeds, chocolate chips, or raisins into the cookies.

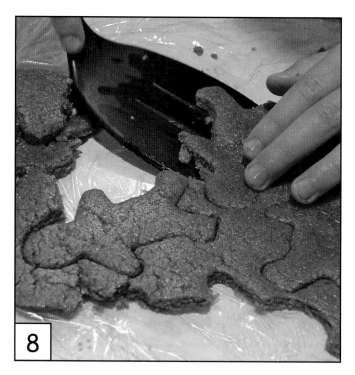

Serving: Eat warm or cool.
Cookies will harden as they cool.

Notes: If a rolling pin or plastic wrap is not available, form dough into small balls and smash down to 1/4-inch thick with palm of hand. It is not necessary to oil the baking sheet for Gingerbread Cookies.

GREEN BEAN CASSEROLE

Yield: 6 servings

Equipment: large bowl, colander, cutting board, paring knife, liquid measuring cup, medium pot with lid, fork, 8-inch square baking dish, big spoon, oven mitts

Ingredients:

1 pound fresh green beans (becomes 4 cups chopped)

1 1/2 cups water

2 cups mushroom soup, canned or carton

1/8 teaspoon ground black pepper, optional

2 cups corn chips or crackers

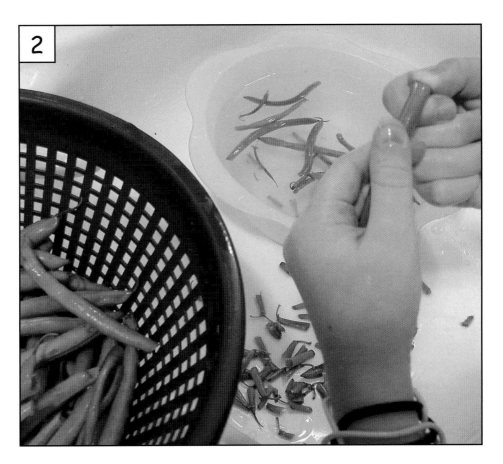

Directions:

1. Wash green beans.

2. Remove stems: Pinch bean with both hands very close to the stem and bend until it breaks. (The stem end is firm; it attached the bean to its plant. The tail end tapers to a point.) Put beans into colander.

3. Cut green beans into 1-inch lengths; cut individually or align 5 beans and cut them simultaneously. Put green beans into pot. Add water.

4. Bring to boil. Reduce heat to low. Place lid on pot.

5. Simmer 10 minutes or until green beans are softened. Remove lid. Allow to cool a few minutes. Drain using colander in the sink; cooking water can be saved for vegetable stock by placing colander in a large bowl prior to draining. Carefully pour green beans into colander.

6. Preheat oven to 375°F. Put green beans in baking dish. Add soup. Add black pepper. Mix. Level top of green beans with back of spoon.

7. Bake for 20 minutes.

Serving: Crumble corn chips until 2 cups reduce to one cup. Sprinkle chips over green beans before serving.

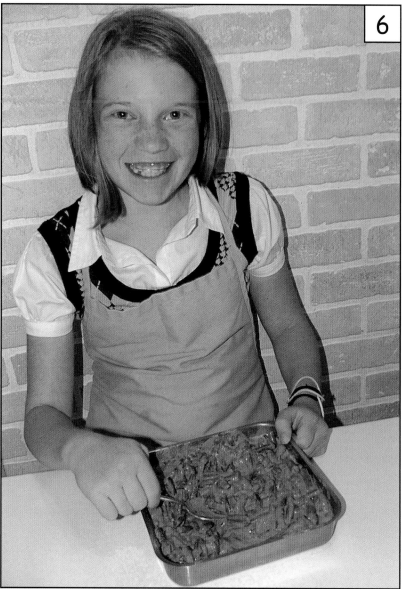

LENTIL VEGETABLE STEW

Yield: 4 servings

Equipment: large pot with lid, dry measuring cups, strainer or colander with holes smaller than a lentil, big colander, liquid measuring cup, vegetable scrub brush, cutting board, chef's knife, large bowl, can opener, small scraping spatula, fork, large spoon

Ingredients:

1 cup lentils, green-brown

3 cups water

1 carrot

1 celery stalk

1 small bunch spinach

1 Tablespoon Italian seasoning
   (mixed herbs)

1 6-ounce can tomato paste

Directions:

1. Put lentils in large pot. Stir lentils with your fingers; look for and remove clods of dirt, tiny stones, and other debris. Add water so lentils are well-covered and finger-swish to wash.

2. Place strainer in sink. Drain lentils into strainer. Repeat washing.

3. Return lentils to pot. Add 3 cups water.

4. Wash and chop carrot. Put carrot in pot.

5. Under running water, brush celery along both sides of stems to remove dirt. Trim the ends. Hold the celery at each cut end of a stalk. Bend the stalk backwards so it

breaks in the middle exposing the strings that run up the outer side of the stalk. Then, pull strings to remove them from stalk, middle to ends. Chop celery similar size to carrot. Add celery to pot.

6. Wash spinach. Cut or rip spinach leaves in half or quarters. Add spinach to pot. Add Italian seasonings.

7. Bring to boil using high heat. Reduce heat, to simmer. Cover with lid. Cook 40 minutes or until lentils and carrots are tender.

8. Wash top of tomato paste can, then open with can opener. Use small scraping spatula to remove tomato paste from can and add to pot. Wash spatula because tomato stains quickly. Use a fork to stir tomato paste into stew water in the pot.

9. Stir the stew with a large spoon.

Note: Other vegetables may be used such as onion, kale, tomatoes, bell peppers, mushrooms, and zucchini.

Q: Why are there stones among lentils?

A: Lentils grow in stony ground. Machines pick the lentils. Stones the same size sometimes get packaged.

FAMILY CHILI

Yield: 8 cups

Equipment: can opener, cutting board, chef's knife, serrated knife, large pot with lid, flat-ended wooden spoon, scraping spatula, serving spoon, liquid measuring cup, dry measuring cups set, measuring spoons set

Ingredients:

1 15-ounce can tomato sauce

1 15-ounce can kidney beans

1 celery stalk

1 small onion

2 Tablespoons olive oil

1 medium tomato

1 cup frozen cut corn

2 cups vegetable stock or water

1 cup textured vegetable protein (TVP)

2 teaspoons chili powder

1 teaspoon cumin powder

Directions:

1. Wash tops of cans of tomato sauce and beans. Open cans. Set aside.

2. Wash celery, onion, and tomato.

3. Break and string the celery. Trim off the ends. Thinly slice celery. Place celery in large pot.

4. Peel, chop, and fry onion (p. 113) with celery and oil in the pot until onion becomes translucent with slightly browned edges. If eyes burn from chopping onion, take a break before frying to wash the cutting board and knife to remove onion residue right away.

5. Add tomato sauce and kidney beans (including liquid) to the pot. Use scraping spatula to remove the end of the can contents.

6. Cut tomato into pieces using the serrated knife. Add tomato to the pot.

7. Measure and add remaining ingredients to the pot: corn, vegetable stock, TVP, chili powder, and cumin powder. Stir.

8. When chili begins to bubble, put lid on pot. Reduce heat to low. Continue cooking for 45 minutes to allow the flavors to blend; stir occasionally.

Serving: Use a ladle to spoon chili into small bowls. Goes great with bread, cornbread, rice, or potatoes.

Note: If TVP is not available, use 1 pound ground meat substitute. Chop it. Do not use vegetable stock or water. Recipe will yield 6 cups.

How to Cut and Fry an Onion

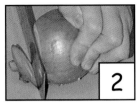

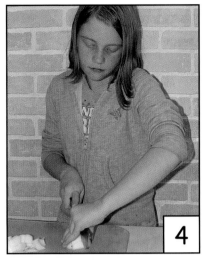

1. Wash onion.

2. Cut off stem end of the onion, leave the root. Stand onion on cut end. Bridge onion and cut in half through the root.

3. Peel onion by removing brown papery outer layer, the thick next layer, and a transparent thin film.

4. Place onion halves flat side down on cutting board. Bridge and cut onion. Rotate onion 90 degrees, cut at least twice to chop onion; cut off root.

5. Put onion in pot. Add oil.

6. Turn on stove vent fan. Set burner to medium-high heat. Stir onion with flat-ended wooden spoon. Fry 5 to 10 minutes until onion is translucent. If oil spatters or smokes, reduce heat.

Caution: Hot oil should sizzle, not smoke. Smoke means heat is too high. Remove from heat and put lid on pot to reduce possibility of fire.

Tricks for crying less: Never touch your face while cooking, especially working with onions. Soak onion in ice water for five minutes after peeling, or at least rewash under cold water. Wear swimming goggles. Try not to put face directly above onion because vapors rise. Use celery or bell pepper instead of onion.

Questions	Answers
1. What are the ends of the onion called?	1. shoot and root
2. What is the homophone to shoot?	2. chute (slide)
3. What is the homonym to shoot?	3. shoot (a gun)
4. What is the homophone to root?	4. route (course)
5. What part of the plant is an onion?	5. bulb

CHOCOMINT PUDDING

Yield: 4 servings

Equipment: small pot, liquid measuring cup, dry measuring cups set, plate, medium pot with lid, measuring spoons set, table knife, small spoon, flat-ended wooden spoon

Ingredients:

1/2 cup water

1 peppermint tea bag or 20 leaves
   fresh peppermint

1/3 cup raw cane sugar

1/4 cup unsweetened cocoa powder

1/4 cup corn starch

2 cups vanilla soymilk

Directions:

1. Pour water into small pot. Bring water to boil. Remove from heat. Place tea bag in the water and cover with lid for at least three minutes to make strong peppermint tea.

2. While tea is steeping, place sugar in medium pot. Add cocoa powder to pot. Add starch. Mix with a small spoon.

3. Use small spoon to remove tea bag (or mint leaves) from tea. Add half of the tea to the dry ingredients.

4. Mix well, smashing any lumps with the back of the spoon against the side of the pot. Add the rest of the tea. Mix again.

5. Add soymilk to chocolate-peppermint mixture. Stir with flat-ended wooden spoon to check that none of the ingredients are stuck to the bottom of the pan.

6. Cook on medium-high heat. Stir constantly with flat-ended wooden spoon, very slowly so it does not splash, while bringing it almost to boil. Be patient - it will take a few minutes.  Scrape the entire bottom of the pot constantly as it heats. Stay with the pot. Remove from heat as soon as it begins to have big bubbles - BEFORE IT RISES UP AND BOILS OVER THE SIDES.

7. Allow to cool uncovered for an hour. Place lid on pot and set it in refrigerator. Chill overnight, a few hours, or until pudding has thickened.

Serving: Ladle pudding into 4 small dishes. Serve with small spoons.

CHOCOLATE CHIP COOKIES

Yield: 15 cookies

Equipment: 2 mixing bowls, dry measuring cups, spoon, table knife, 2 plates, fork, 2 mixing spoons, measuring spoons set, baking sheet, parchment paper or cooking spray, scraping spatula, oven mitts, cooling racks, lifting spatula

Ingredients:

1/4 cup soy margarine

2/3 cup raw cane sugar

1 small banana

1 teaspoon vanilla extract

1 cup whole wheat pastry flour

1 teaspoon baking powder

1 cup semisweet non-dairy chocolate chips

Directions:

1. Set margarine out in the kitchen a few minutes to soften.
2. Place measured margarine in a mixing bowl. Add sugar to the bowl. Mash margarine with fork. Mix with sugar until it looks like frosting.
3. Peel and mash banana. Add mashed banana to sugar mixture. Add vanilla. Mix well.
4. Put flour in other mixing bowl. Add the baking powder. Mix using a dry mixing spoon.
5. Pour flour mixture into banana mixture. Mix thoroughly. Add chocolate chips. Mix again.

5

6. Preheat oven to 375°F. Place a piece of parchment paper on baking sheet (or oil the baking sheet). Drop cookie dough by heaping tablespoons onto parchment, leaving at least an inch space between cookies. Use scraping spatula to scrape the end of the dough from the mixing bowl.

7. Bake cookies for 12 to 15 minutes. Cookies should still be soft, but not wet. Lightly browned on the edges is good. They will harden as they cool.

8. Allow cookies to cool a few minutes. Using lifting spatula, slide cookies onto cooling rack to continue cooling.

Serving: Eat warm or cool. Share with other people...or not.

Notes: A small ice cream scoop with a spring-loaded release makes it easy to place cookies on the baking sheet instead of the heaping tablespoon.
For crunchy cookies, air cool completely for a few hours. For soft cookies, store in an airtight container as soon as cooled to room temperature.

WHOLE WHEAT PIE CRUST

Use for Pumpkin Pie and Apple Pie

Yield: one 8-inch round pie crust

Equipment: 8-inch diameter pie pan, dry measuring cups, spoon, table knife, measuring spoons set, liquid measuring cup, fork, oven mitts

Ingredients:

1 cup whole wheat pastry flour

1/4 teaspoon salt

1/4 cup vegetable oil

3 Tablespoons cold water

2 **Directions:**

1. Preheat oven to 375°F. Place flour in pie pan. Add salt. Mix.

2. Measure oil in liquid measuring cup. Add water to the oil in the cup.

3. Beat oil and water with fork until emulsified.

4. Pour liquid over flour.

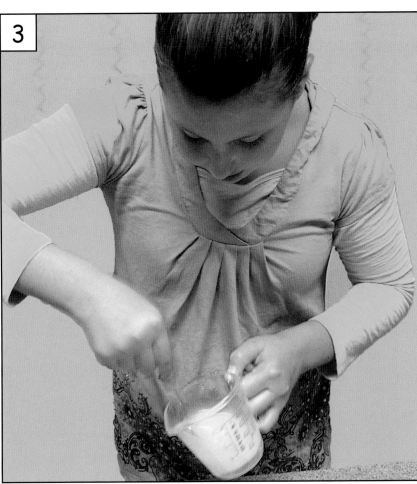

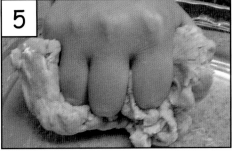

5. Mix until well-blended using fork, then hands.

6. Press into shape with fingers. Prick at least 20 times with fork on sides and bottom of crust to poke holes that allow air to escape while baking.

7. Bake for 7 minutes to firm the crust slightly before adding fillings. It will not be ready to eat. Follow pie recipe for further baking instructions.

Note: Store flour in freezer. Cold flour produces the best results. Ice cold water may also be used.

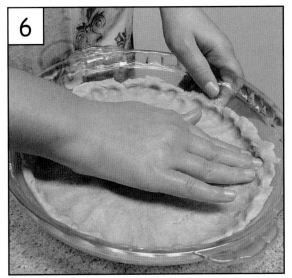

PUMPKIN PIE

Yield: one 8-inch pie

Equipment: liquid measuring cup, measuring spoons set, table knife, large mixing bowl, fork, large spoon, can opener, scraping spatula, oven mitts

Ingredients:

1 1/2 Tablespoons cornstarch

1 Tablespoon pumpkin pie spices

1/8 teaspoon salt, optional (half fill 1/4 teaspoon)

3/4 cup vanilla soymilk (1/4 cup + 1/2 cup)

1 15-ounce can pumpkin

1/2 cup maple syrup or agave

1 8-inch Whole Wheat Pie Crust (in pan)

Directions:

1. Preheat oven to 375°F.
2. Place cornstarch in large mixing bowl. Add spices. Add salt. Mix.
3. Add 1/4 cup of the soymilk. Mix until there are no lumps; squish lumps with the back of spoon against the bowl.

120

4. Add remaining soymilk. Add pumpkin, use scraping spatula to get pumpkin out of the end of the can. Add maple syrup. Mix slowly so it doesn't splatter.

4

5

5. Pour or spoon pumpkin filling into a prepared pie crust. Spread top flat with scraping (spreading) spatula.

6. Bake for 45 minutes.

Note: Pumpkin pie spices are a usually sold together as mix of cinnamon, ginger, nutmeg and allspice.

Serving: Slice into 8 pieces with a knife. Use a triangular lifting spatula under each slice to serve. Have plates next to the pie so you can serve each piece easily.

APPLE PIE

Yield: one 8-inch pie

Equipment: cutting board, paring knife, large liquid measuring cup, measuring spoons set, 1/2-cup dry measuring cup, table knife, large mixing bowl, small bowl, fork, large spoon, oven mitts

Ingredients:

3 large (or 4 small) apples, mixed varieties

1 Tablespoon cornstarch

1 Tablespoon cinnamon

1/2 cup grape jelly

2 Tablespoons water

1 8-inch Whole Wheat Pie Crust (in pan)

Directions:

1. Preheat oven to 375°F.

2. Wash apples. Peeling is optional. Core and chop 2 apples using the tic-tac-toe method to yield 3 cups of apples. Place apples in the mixing bowl.

2

3. Add cornstarch. Add cinnamon. Mix to distribute dry ingredients among the apple pieces.

4. Put the jelly in small bowl. Add water. Mix gently by mashing it with a fork until jelly is not lumpy. Pour half (1/4 cup) of the jelly sauce into the apples. Mix.

5. Put apple filling in a prepared pie crust. Scrape bowl with spatula. Lightly press down fruit into the pan with spoon.

6. Core and slice the remaining apple into crescents 1/8- to 1/4-inch thick. Arrange slices on top of the pie in a flower-shape with slightly overlapping petals. Keep all the slices inside the crust edge.

7. Spoon the remaining jelly sauce onto the apple slices.

8. Spread the jelly sauce over the slices.

9. Bake for 45 minutes.

CARROT CAKE

Yield: one 9-inch cake

Equipment: dry measuring cups, table knife, 2 plates, measuring spoons set, 2 mixing bowls, large spoon, vegetable scrub brush, paring knife, cutting board, peeler, grater, liquid measuring cup, medium strainer, medium bowl, 9-inch springform tube pan, paper towel, whisk, scraping spatula, oven mitts

Ingredients:

Dry ingredients:

1 1/3 cup whole wheat pastry flour

1 cup whole wheat bread flour

2 Tablespoons ground flaxseed

1 Tablespoon cinnamon

2 teaspoons nutmeg

1 teaspoon cornstarch

1 teaspoon baking soda

1/2 teaspoon salt

1/2 cup chopped walnuts (p. 126)

Wet ingredients:

To oil pan: 2 teaspoons oil

2 large carrots

1 cup crushed pineapple

1 cup maple syrup or agave

1/4 cup vegetable oil

Directions:

1. Place all the dry ingredients in large mixing bowl. Mix. Set aside.

2. Preheat oven to 350°F. Put 2 teaspoons oil into assembled pan. Wipe oil around inside (bottom, sides, center) of pan with paper towel. Set aside.

3. Scrub carrots. Peel and grate carrots which should measure approximately 1 1/2 cups. Put carrots in second mixing bowl.

4. Put strainer over medium bowl. Put pineapple in strainer to drain. Do not smash out additional juice; leave somewhat wet. Put drained pineapple into the carrot bowl. Pour juice from bowl into glass for chef to drink.

5. Place syrup in the medium bowl. Add oil. Whisk until it emulsifies.

6. Add syrup/oil to the carrot/pineapple mixture. Mix.

7. Add dry mixture to the wet mixture. Mix until there is no dry flour in the bowl.

8. Spoon batter into pan. Scrape bowl with spatula. Smooth top slightly with spatula.

9. Bake for 40 minutes or until the cake passes a toothpick test (p. 126).

10. Allow cake to cool in the pan. Take off outer ring of the pan. Use scraping spatula between cake and bottom of pan to loosen cake.

11. Put plate on top and flip cake out of pan onto plate. It can be reflipped using a second plate like a sandwich.

Serving: Top with Coconut Vanilla Icing (p. 127), or a fruit jam such as apricot or peach with a sprinkle of shredded coconut, or a side of vanilla ice cream.

How to Chop Walnuts

To make 1/2 cup chopped walnuts, start with 2/3 cup nuts. Use cutting board and chef's knife. Keep second hand flat on top of knife when chopping nuts. Use technique similar to mincing herbs: chop, gather pieces, chop.

The Toothpick Test

1. Hold toothpick. Insert a clean toothpick halfway into the center of cake. Pull it out.

2. Look at toothpick. If cake sticks to toothpick, cake needs further baking. If toothpick remains clean, cake is done. For cake in a tube pan, use halfway between cake edges as a center.

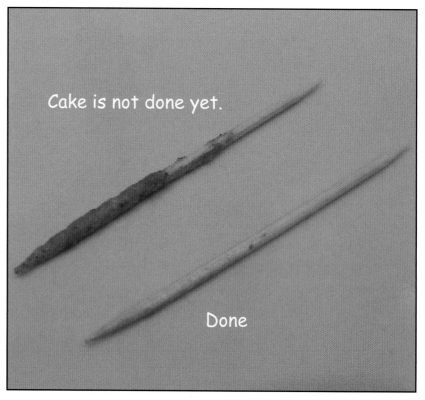

Cake is not done yet.

Done

COCONUT VANILLA ICING

Yield: 1 1/2 cups

Skill learned: icing a cake

Equipment: 2-cup liquid measuring cup, fork, jar, measuring spoons set, table knife, medium pot, spoon, wooden flat-ended spoon

Ingredients:

1 cup canned unsweetened coconut milk

2 Tablespoons cornstarch

1/2 cup maple syrup or agave

1 teaspoon vanilla extract

Directions:

1. Open can of coconut milk. Pour into measuring cup. Mix until smooth before measuring amount needed. Pour excess in jar and refrigerate for future.

2. Place 1/4 cup of coconut milk in pot. Add cornstarch. Mix until there are no lumps by smashing lumps against the side of the pot with back of a spoon.

3. Add remaining 3/4 cup of coconut milk. Mix. Add syrup. Add vanilla. Mix.

4. Cook on medium-high heat. Stir constantly, scraping bottom in circles and figure eights with wooden flat-ended spoon until icing thickens.

5. Allow to cool, then refrigerate.

Serving: When cooled, ice the Carrot Cake using a spreading spatula.

Note: If using sweetened coconut milk, 1 1/2 cups coconut milk may be used in place of 1 cup unsweetened coconut milk and 1/2 cup syrup. Do not use carton coconut milk because it is watery compared with the full-fat canned.

SPINACH TOFU LASAGNA

Yield: 12 servings (family size)

Equipment: 8x12-inch casserole pan, small pillowcase or salad spinner for fresh spinach or scissors and large strainer for frozen spinach, cutting board, chef's knife, can opener, mixing spoon, dry measuring cups, paring knife, paper towels, cloth towel, spoon, large mixing bowl, measuring spoons set, table knife, peeler, grater, plate, baking sheet, lifting spatula

Ingredients:

2 teaspoons oil (to oil pan)

1 small bunch fresh spinach, approximately 1/2 pound, or use 1 pound frozen and thawed

1 29-ounce can (approximately 3 1/4 cups) tomato sauce

8 lasagna noodles, uncooked

1 1/2 pounds firm or regular tofu

1 cup soy mayonnaise

1/4 cup nutritional yeast, optional

2 Tablespoons Italian seasonings (mixed herbs), optional

1 or 2 carrots

Directions:

1. Lightly oil casserole pan. Wipe oil around inside of pan with paper towel. Set aside.

For fresh spinach:

2A. Wash spinach in warm water which will begin to wilt spinach. (Wilt means to become limp or droopy.) Spin water off spinach. Remove spinach stems if desired. Chop half of the spinach. Cover the bottom of the pan with the chopped spinach. Chop the other half of spinach and set aside.

For frozen spinach:

2B. Thaw spinach at room temperature by planning ahead, or by putting unopened package in warm water. Put some of the spinach in a strainer. Gently press spinach to drain off water; put spinach in large bowl. Repeat until all spinach is pressed. Cover the bottom of the pan with half the thawed spinach.

3. Open can of tomato sauce. Pour 3/4 cup of the sauce on the spinach. This is easily done using the 1/4 cup dry measuring cup as a dipper if the sauce is in a large can. Spread with spoon. This will further wilt the spinach to take up less space.

4. Put 4 of the uncooked lasagna noodles on the sauce as the next layer.

5. Lay the remaining spinach on the lasagna. Spread 1 cup of the sauce on the spinach. Make sure sauce gets to the edges.

6. Open tofu packages. Drain, rinse, and drain. Cut tofu into 1-inch thick slices. Do the blotting tofu process with towels until tofu begins to squish.

7. Crumble tofu in the bowl by squishing it through your fist. Rinse hands.

8. Measure soy mayonnaise using the spoon to get it in and out of the 1-cup dry measuring cup into the bowl. Add nutritional yeast and Italian seasonings to the tofu. Mix well.

9. Preheat oven to 350°F.

Top of pan
Sauce
Carrot
Tofu
Lasagna
Tofu
Sauce
Spinach
Lasagna
Sauce
Spinach
Bottom of pan

10. Put half of the tofu mixture by small spoonfuls on the sauce as the next layer. Gently push the tofu around to make it more evenly spread.

11. Place remaining 4 lasagna noodles on the tofu. Spread remaining tofu on top of lasagna.

12. Wash, peel, and grate carrot. Scatter carrot on the tofu.

13. Top with remaining sauce (about 1 1/2 cups). Spread sauce generously over all the lasagna. Make sure all the noodles are pushed under the surface so they will cook without drying or burning. Nothing should hang over the edge.

14. Place baking sheet in oven. Place pan on baking sheet in case bubbling sauce overflows as it cooks. Bake uncovered for 60 minutes or until lasagna noodles are tender to a fork.

Note: If the pan is heavy, ask an adult to put it in and out of oven.

Serving: Cut with a chef's knife. Serve using a lifting spatula.

VEGGIE WRAPS

This is a great activity for a group of 4 kids (or one ambitious person). Each kid can pick two wrap filling ingredients to prepare and share. Some ingredients are easy, others are harder. Makes 8 wraps.

Adult recipe books will not tell you the equipment and some of the preparation steps. If you do not remember how to prepare lettuce, rice, tomato, carrot, and green beans, refer back to earlier pages. Use steps 1-5 of Green Bean Casserole, but do not chop the beans. Use of deli paper or plastic wrap is optional.

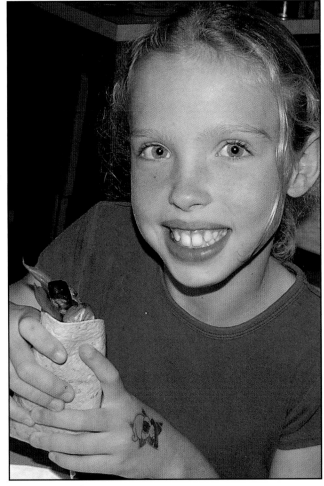

Ingredients:

8 wheat flour tortilla (large, round)

4 leaves lettuce, washed

3/4 cup hummus

1/2 cup Brown Rice, cooked

16 Eggplant Strips (p. 133)

1 large tomato, washed and diced

1 carrot, grated

1/2 cup Flavored Mushrooms (p. 134)

24 green beans, steamed

Directions:

1. Put tortilla on plate. Put half a lettuce leaf on top 2/3 of tortilla. Spread 1 or 2 tablespoons hummus on the lettuce.

2. Add the fillings you want such as 1 tablespoon brown rice, two strips eggplant, 1 tablespoon diced tomatoes,
   1 tablespoon grated carrot,
   1 tablespoon mushrooms,
   and 3 green beans.

3. Fold in sides of lettuce.

4. Fold tortilla up one third (1/3) from the bottom. Fold in the sides.

Note: If Veggie Wraps are being premade for a large group or travel, use deli paper or plastic wrap to hold them in shape. Put deli paper on plate with corner on top. After making the wrap, fold deli paper up and around wrap. Turn paper down from top to eat.

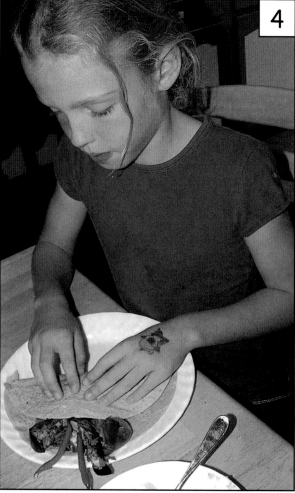

Eggplant Strips

Equipment: 8x12-inch casserole pan, cutting board, serrated knife, whisk or fork, oven mitts, lifting spatula

Ingredients:

2 Tablespoons soy sauce

2 teaspoons olive oil

1/2 teaspoon curry powder

1/4 teaspoon mixed dried herbs such as
   Italian seasoning

1 small eggplant

Directions:

1. Put soy sauce, oil, curry powder, and herbs into pan. Slightly lift one corner of the pan so everything flows to the opposite corner. Mix with whisk or fork.

2. Wash eggplant. Use serrated knife in a sawing motion to cut stem end off eggplant. Then cut eggplant in half lengthwise. Put flat side on cutting board and cut in half widthwise. Cut into strips 1/2-inch thick by 1 inch wide by approximately 4 inches long.

3. Preheat oven to 375°F. Place eggplant in casserole pan. Turn eggplant strips over to coat.

4. Bake for 20 minutes or until brown and tender when poked with fork. Allow to cool. Use lifting spatula to remove eggplant from pan.

Flavored Mushrooms

Equipment: cutting board, paring knife, small pot

Ingredients:

8 mushrooms

1/2 Tablespoon olive oil

1/2 Tablespoon soy sauce

Directions:

1. Wash mushrooms.
2. Place one mushroom on cutting board. Slice mushroom in half.
3. Place new flat side on cutting board. Cut mushroom into slices approximately 1/8-inch thick.
4. Put oil in pot. Add soy sauce. Cook on medium-high heat. When oil begins to sizzle, add mushrooms. Reduce heat to medium-low. Place lid on pot. Cook for 10 minutes.

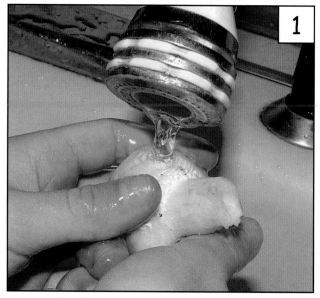

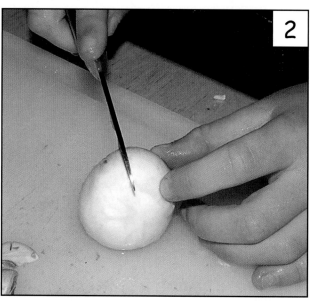

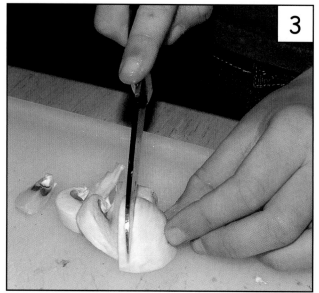

Level Four:
Using a Blender

Safe Blender Usage and Cleanup

Blenders vary greatly. Learn about blender speeds and functions specific to the brand of blender used. Be sure the goblet and goblet base (bottom cap) are not cross threaded; they must be screwed together tightly. Settle the goblet base firmly on the motor base. Lid must be correctly in place. **Locate the "off" button before turning the blender on.** Start on slow speed before using high speed. Never run a blender with a spoon in it! **Keep fingers out of blender when blender is on!**

Safe Effective Blender Cleanup

1. Remove food contents.

2. Half-fill goblet with water and add a drop of dish soap. Put lid on firmly.

3. Blend. Turn off. Remove from base.

4. Take goblet to sink. Sponge or brush inside and outside of goblet. Clean the lid.

5. Adults may opt to remove goblet base/bottom cap for cleaning. Brush blades, gasket, goblet base, and threads of the goblet.

6. Rinse all goblet parts and lid.

7. Unplug base. Never immerse base in water. Wipe base clean using a sponge or damp cloth.

ALMOND MILK

Yield: 1 cup

Skills learned:

blanching, blender basics

Equipment: liquid measuring cup, small pot, colander, blender, jar with lid

Ingredients:

1 cup water

24 raw almonds

1 cup cold water

Directions:

1. Place 1 cup of water in pot. Bring to a boil.

2. Count almonds into measuring cup. Pour almonds into the boiling water. Turn off heat. Allow almonds to soak for 5 minutes.

3. Place colander in sink and pour almonds into colander. Run cold water from faucet on almonds.

4. Squeeze rounded end of each almond between thumb and fingers to remove skin; point almond back into the colander because almonds tend to fly quickly. Rinse almonds with cool water.

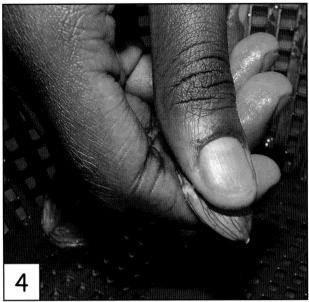

4. Place almonds in blender with 1 cup cold water. Place lid firmly on blender goblet. Place goblet securely on the blender base.

5. Blend until smooth. Most blenders have a variety of settings: begin with a low speed, then go to a higher speed. Turn off blender.

6. Pour almond milk into a jar. Put lid on jar and store in refrigerator. Remember to clean the blender when finished.

Serving: Shake jar before use. Can be poured into a measuring cup for easier pouring into small glasses. Tastes great on hot cereal such as oatmeal. Almond milk can be sweetened to taste: add a few pitted dates before blending or mix in a teaspoon of maple syrup anytime.

Note: Blanch means briefly drop a food into boiling water OR make white. This recipe does both.

PEACH BANANA SMOOTHIE

Yield: 2 servings

Equipment: blender, cutting board, paring knife, liquid measuring cup, 2 glasses

Ingredients:

2 peaches

1/2 cup soymilk

2 frozen bananas (p. 142)

Directions:

1. Wash peaches. Pit and quarter peaches like you would an avocado. Some peaches have cling pits which are hard to remove.

2. Chop peach. Place peach pieces in blender. Rinse hands so blender buttons do not get all sticky.

3. Add soymilk to blender. Put lid on blender tightly. Place blender securely on its base.

4. Blend until smooth, using low then higher speeds. Turn off blender.

5. Break frozen bananas in half or more pieces. If they don't break easily, let them thaw a few minutes.

6. Add bananas to blender. Rinse hands. Replace lid tightly.

7. Blend on a medium setting or adjust for the power of the blender. Blend until you do not hear or see lumps, burping blender if necessary (p. 142).

Serving: Pour into glasses and share with a friend.

Note: Smoothies will also work if the peaches are frozen (pitted, chopped) instead of the bananas. If nothing is frozen, the smoothie will not be as thick and cold. Other fruits such as strawberries or pears can be substituted for peaches to create different flavored smoothies.

Freezing Bananas

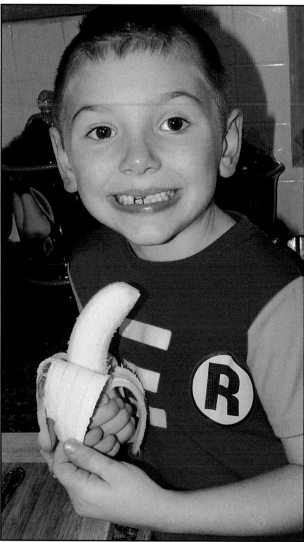

Frozen bananas are great to have available throughout the summer. Plan ahead. Peel bananas and put them in a plastic bag. Put the bag in the freezer overnight or a few hours.

Burping the Blender

If it does not blend smoothly, turn off the blender and use a long-handled spoon to push ingredients toward the blades. Sometimes an air bubble will release. This is known as burping the blender. **Be sure to remove the spoon before turning on the blender again!**

Replace the lid and try blending again.

If blending is difficult because mixture is too thick to move, turn off blender. Add one tablespoon of water and burp again to permit water to get to the blades. Replace lid. Try blending again.

MUSHROOM SOUP

Eat or use in Green Bean Casserole.

Yield: 3 cups

Equipment: cutting board, paring knife, liquid measuring cup, medium pot, blender, big spoon, scraping spatula

Ingredients:

2 Tablespoons vegetable oil

1 large onion

10 ounces (4 1/2 cups) mushrooms

1/2 teaspoon salt

1 cup water or vegetable stock

3/4 cup soymilk (plain, unsweetened preferred) or ricemilk

2 slices whole wheat bread

Directions:

1. Put oil in pot. Wash, peel, and chop onion. Put onion in pot. Put lid on pot to keep in the onion vapors. Rinse cutting board, knife, and hands to remove onion residue (less crying).

2. Wash mushrooms with your fingers under a small stream of running water. Put mushrooms in colander. Slice mushroom caps and stems. Add mushrooms to pot. Add salt which will sweat liquid for cooking from the vegetables. Put lid on pot.

3. Cook on medium-high heat for 10 minutes. Reduce heat to medium-low; simmer for 10 more minutes.

4. Remove lid from pot. Cool for 5 minutes.

5. Spoon half of the mushrooms and onions into the blender. Spoon or pour most of the cooking liquid into the blender. Add soymilk. Add only 1/2 cup of the water, retaining the option for thicker soup.

6. Break bread slices and add to blender. Blend until smooth. Gradually add remaining water to thin soup if desired.

7. Pour blended mushroom soup into the pot with remaining mushrooms and onions. Scrape blender with spatula. Stir.

8. If reheating is necessary, use medium heat, stirring and scraping bottom of pan.

Note: Mushroom flavor will intensify over time and the soup will thicken.

By now you know to put lid securely on blender, put blender firmly on base, find a speed that will blend it (low, then higher), and turn off blender. These directions no longer appear in the recipes.

HUMMUS

Use homemade hummus next time you make Veggie Wraps!

Yield: 2 cups

Skills learned: blender experience with thick contents

Equipment: can opener, liquid measuring cup, blender, measuring spoons, paring knife, cutting board, long handled teaspoon, scraping spatula, bowl

Ingredients:

1 15-ounce can chickpeas (garbanzos)

1/2 small raw onion

3 Tablespoons lemon juice (1 lemon)

2 1/2 Tablespoons olive oil

2 1/2 Tablespoons sesame tahini (roasted preferred)

1/8 teaspoon onion powder

1/8 teaspoon garlic powder

Directions:

1. Determine whether you are using tahini from a new can. If so, see Mixing Tahini (p. 147). If not, proceed directly to step 2.

2. Wash top of chickpea can. Open can. Place can lid on top of can to hold in chickpeas while draining liquid into liquid measuring cup. Pour chickpeas into the blender.

3. Wash, peel, and chop onion. Add to blender. Wash knife and cutting board.

4. Juice lemon, remove seeds, and add juice to blender. Add olive oil, tahini (if not already in blender), onion powder, garlic powder, and 2 Tablespoons chickpea water.

5. Place blender on base; put lid on blender tightly. Blend until smooth. You may add more chickpea water in small quantities to help it blend.

6. Pour hummus into bowl. Use a scraping spatula to remove the remaining hummus from the blender.

Serving: Use as a dip for carrot sticks, celery sticks, broccoli, cauliflower, cherry tomatoes, crackers, or toasted pita bread. Put on steamed vegetables as a cheesy topping. Slather on bread as a sandwich spread, then add lettuce and tomato.

Variation: Instead of onion,

onion powder, and garlic powder, use 1/4 teaspoon dried dill weed or 1/4 teaspoon ground cumin or 1 roasted red bell pepper or 1/8 teaspoon salt.

Mixing Tahini

Tahini (made from sesame seeds) has a tendency to separate, even more than peanut butter does. Therefore, tahini should be mixed prior to using. Although it can be done by hand with a fork, it is much easier to use the blender the first time.

1. Shake unopened tahini can and listen. Can you hear the oil sloshing? The oil will be at the top of the can if it was stored with the top facing up. Unless you have stored the tahini upside down for a month, opening it upside down will make it easier to remove tahini from the can's bottom surface. Rinse and dry surface you will be opening. Open can. If tahini comes in a jar, you will open the top.

2. Pour tahini oil into blender and spoon in the solid tahini.

3. Blend until smooth.

4. Return tahini to its original container. Use scraping spatula to get most of the tahini from the blender (see note).

Note: The tahini that remains before scraping may be close to the amount needed to use in hummus, making scraping/measuring unnecessary. Preparing hummus in the blender after blending tahini helps loosen the tahini so the blender is easier to clean.

BANANA ICE CREAM

Yield: 8 servings

Equipment: blender, 1/4-cup dry measuring cup, spoon, scraping spatula, mixing bowl, 8 3-ounce paper cups, aluminum foil

Ingredients:

5 bananas

1/4 cup raw cashew nuts

1/4 cup toasted carob powder
   (optional, see note)

1/4 cup raisins (optional)

1/4 cup shelled unsalted raw sunflower
   seeds (optional)

Directions:

1. Stand blender goblet directly on counter. Peel bananas and put them into the blender. Hold blender firmly with one hand and smash down the bananas with your fist. Your hand should not be near the blades, but will smash the bananas into the blades. Rinse hands.

2. Blend until smooth. Burp the blender if necessary.

3. Add cashews. Blend until smooth.

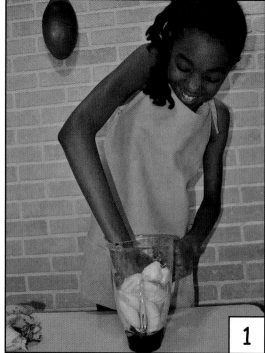

4

4. Add carob. Blend until evenly brown throughout.

5. Pour into mixing bowl. Use scraping spatula to remove blender contents; be careful not to stick the spatula into the point of a blade.

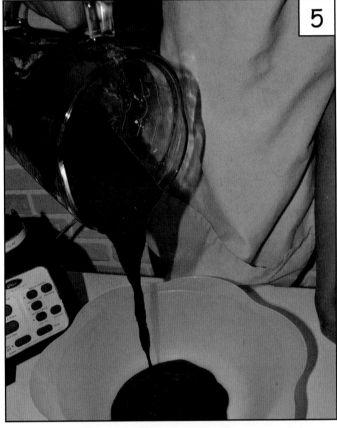

5

6. Add raisins and sunflower seeds to the bowl. Mix.

7. Put mixture into eight 3-ounce paper cups. Cover each cup with a piece of aluminum foil.

8. Place cups in freezer overnight or at least 4 hours, depending on the temperature of your freezer.

Serving: Allow to thaw 5 minutes or until it can be eaten with a sturdy spoon or you can rip cup and bite.

Note: Instead of carob, use 1/4 cup cocoa powder and 2 Tablespoons maple syrup or other sweetener.

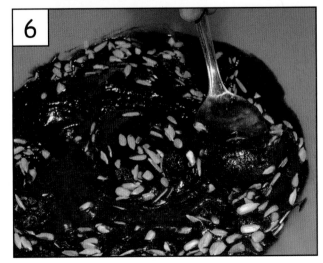

6

CHOCORANGE CUPCAKES

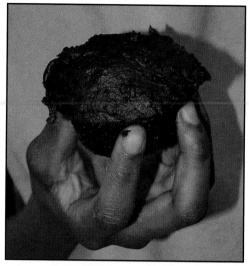

Yield: 12 cupcakes

Equipment: 12-hole muffin tin, paper towels, chopping board, paring knife, table knife, dry measuring cup set, wet measuring cup, measuring spoons set, large spoon, blender, mixing bowl, scraping spatula, cooling rack (optional)

Ingredients:

2 teaspoons corn oil or other vegetable oil

1/2 pound regular firm tofu

1 cup orange juice

1 cup granulated cane juice or other sweetener

1/3 cup unsweetened cocoa powder

1 Tablespoon baking soda

2 teaspoons dried orange peel

1/2 teaspoon dried ginger powder

1 1/3 cups whole wheat pastry flour or unbleached flour

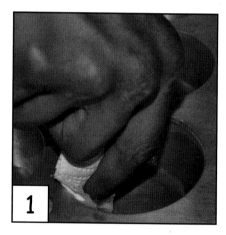

Directions:

1. Put a drop of the oil in each of the muffin tin's cups. Spread it around with a paper towel.

   If using a non-stick tin, skip this step.

2. Preheat oven to 350°F.

3. Drain and rinse tofu. Cut to 1/2-pound size and store the remainder.

4. Put all ingredients except flour in blender.

5. Blend until smooth. If cocoa sticks to sides of blender, turn it off; use scraping spatula to scrape the cocoa and blend again. Pour into bowl.

6. Add flour to bowl. Mix just until there are no lumps.

7. Put batter into muffin tins. Use a paper towel to wipe off anything that spills on the muffin tin (so it doesn't burn or run over the edge while baking).

8. Bake for 20 minutes. Let cool.

9. Flip onto cooling rack or paper towels. If the cupcakes don't come out easily, smack the tin or gently pull them out.

Serve: Top with Chocorange Icing (p. 152).

CHOCORANGE ICING

Yield: icing for one cake or 12 iced Chocorange Cupcakes and plenty to lick!

Equipment: blender, medium pot, flat-ended spoon

Ingredients:

1 cup orange juice

2/3 unsweetened cocoa powder

1 cup granulated cane juice or other dry
  sweetener

1/3 cup cornstarch

1/2 teaspoon dried ginger powder

4

3

Directions:

1. Put all ingredients in the blender.

2. Blend until smooth. Pour into pot.

3. Heat on medium-high. Stir constantly, scraping bottom until the mixture thickens. It will take a few minutes and then thicken suddenly.

4. Allow to cool before spreading on cupcakes.

Congratulations!

You have now completed the entire recipe book!

We hope you keep enjoying your homemade foods. You can make the things you learned in this book over and over again. When you feel ready for a new challenge, try these easy adult recipe books by the authors:

Healthy Hearty Helpings by Anne Dinshah

Simple recipes for students and other busy people abound in this treasure trove of ideas to produce for yourself or for your family. Many dishes are great for a potluck.

The 4-Ingredient Vegan by Maribeth Abrams and Anne Dinshah

Each recipe has only 4 ingredients, not counting water, oil, salt, or pepper. Easy, quick, and delicious recipes will have you creating scrumptious entrees, salads, soups, side dishes, beverages, and desserts with maximum flavor.

The Vegan Kitchen by Freya Dinshah

The first U.S. recipe book to use "vegan" in its title, this timeless classic gives a foundation of simple fare from before you could buy vegan convenience foods. Originally published in 1965, it is now in the 13th edition.

Adults and teens may also enjoy *Dating Vegans: Recipes for Relationships* by Anne Dinshah. This book is for everyone in a relationship vegan-with-a-nonvegan, or anyone who has a vegan friend. Social issues are boldly tackled with stories from real people, insights, and over 50 easy recipes. Better than a romance novel whisking readers away to fantasy, *Dating Vegans* is a catalyst for reevaluating interactions.

About the Authors

Anne Dinshah invited 26 children to learn and create techniques for this book. She enjoyed developing kid-friendly language with them, photographing their efforts, and sharing the tasting tasks.

Anne has a bachelor of arts from the University of Notre Dame and a master of education from the University of Texas at Austin. She is a rowing coach by profession which often requires travel, but she officially resides in a stone and timber-frame writer's cabin she built with the help of many friends in western New York.

Anne credits her mother Freya for instilling in her a love of cooking and her father Jay for a love of eating delicious homemade food. Her son Clint makes cameo appearances in this book and loves to scrub potatoes.

Freya Dinshah provided the concept for the book, supplied the majority of the recipes, and guided the project. For several years she has volunteered at the Newfield Terrace Community Action Organization after-school program. Freya is currently serving as nutrition educator and teaches basic cooking skills to children ages 6 to 18.

She has been a key organizer for local and national events to encourage compassionate, healthful living. Freya has taught cooking classes to people of all ages for over 40 years.

Freya resides in southern New Jersey where she works full-time for a nonprofit organization. She feels fortunate to live in an area where local produce is abundant. She has two adult children, Daniel and Anne, who both learned to cook under her guidance.

Anne and Freya

Anne, Freya, and Jay Dinshah
shelling lima beans for dinner in September 1979

Certificate of Accomplishment

_____ (name)

is a competent

LEVEL ONE CHEF

for recipes from

Apples, Bean Dip, and Carrot Cake

_____ (adult supervisor) _____ (date)

Certificate of Accomplishment

_____ (name)

is a competent

LEVEL TWO CHEF

for recipes from

Apples, Bean Dip, and Carrot Cake

_____ (adult supervisor) _____ (date)

This page is the reverse side of the certificates for level one & two.

Certificate of Accomplishment

_____ (name)

is a competent

LEVEL THREE CHEF

for recipes from

Apples, Bean Dip, and Carrot Cake

_____ (adult supervisor) _____ (date)

Certificate of Accomplishment

_____ (name)

is a competent

LEVEL FOUR CHEF

for recipes from

Apples, Bean Dip, and Carrot Cake

_____ (adult supervisor) _____ (date)

This page is the reverse side of the certificates for level three & four.